thinking
creatively at work

thinking creatively at work

A SOURCEBOOK

Premilla D'Cruz

Response
Business books from SAGE
Los Angeles ■ London ■ New Delhi ■ Singapore
www.sagepublications.com

First published in 2008 by

Response Books
Business books from SAGE
B1/I-1 Mohan Cooperative Industrial Area
Mathura Road, New Delhi 110 044, India

SAGE Publications Inc
2455 Teller Road
Thousand Oaks, California 91320, USA

SAGE Publications Ltd
1 Oliver's Yard, 55 City Road
London EC1Y 1SP, United Kingdom

SAGE Publications Asia-Pacific Pte Ltd
33 Pekin Street
#02-01 Far East Square
Singapore 048763

Published by Vivek Mehra for Response Books, typeset in 10.5/13pt Minion by Star Compugraphics Private Limited, Delhi and printed at Chaman Enterprises, New Delhi.

Library of Congress Cataloging-in-Publication Data Available

ISBN: 978-81-7829-853-5 (PB)

The SAGE Team: Sugata Ghosh, Meena Chakravorty, Amrita Saha and Trinankur Banerjee

To Ernest,

for being the wind beneath my wings, through the years

Contents

List of Tables and Figures

Table

Figures

List of Abbreviations

ADB	Asian Development Bank
AVP	Assistant Vice President
BIFR	Board of Industrial and Financial Reconstruction
BJP	Bharatiya Janata Party
BMS	Bharatiya Mazdoor Sangh
BOT	Build Operate Transfer
CCTL	Chennai Container Terminal Limited
CD	Compact Disc
CEO	Chief Executive Officer
CoPT	Cochin Port Trust
CPEO	Cochin Port Employees Organization
CPSA	Cochin Port Staff Association
CRM	Cold Rolling Mill
CSR	Corporate Social Responsibility
DPA	Dubai Ports Authority
DPI	Dubai Ports International
EQ	Evocative Question
ETP	Electrolytic Tinplate Plant
FDI	Foreign Direct Investment
FF	Force Fit
FMCG	Fast Moving Consumer Goods
HDP	Hot Dip Plant
HR	Human Resources
HRM	Human Resource Management
ICTT	International Container Transshipment Terminal
ID Act	Industrial Disputes Act
IDBI	Industrial Development Bank of India
INR	Indian National Rupee
IIM	Indian Institute of Management
IIT	Indian Institute of Technology
IT	Information Technology

ITES	Information Technology Enabled Services
KRAs	Key Result Areas
LDF	Left Democratic Front
MP	Member of Parliament
NDA	National Democratic Alliance
OD	Organization Development
PAG	Problem As Given
PAU	Problem As Understood
RFP	Request for Proposals
RGCT	Rajiv Gandhi Container Terminal
SEZ	Special Economic Zone
SPV	Special Purpose Vehicle
TEU	Twenty Foot Equivalent Units
TMBP	Tin Mill Black Plate
UPA	United Progressive Alliance
UTI	Unit Trust of India
VP	Vice President
VRS	Voluntary Retirement Scheme

Acknowledgements

My tryst with the world of creativity and cognition began as an undergraduate student of psychology, and bringing this dimension into creativity training for participants with a management/ business administration background has served to enrich the endeavor. This book is the outcome of my work as an academic in the field of creativity and cognition, and of my experiences as a trainer in creative thinking. My gratitude to Jennie Mendes, for stimulating and nurturing in me an abiding interest in cognitive psychology and to S. Jeyavelu for an insightful discussion on creativity training.

Vinodini Raveendran, Bhupinder Arora and Pandurangan Rao have helped me immensely in typing various materials related to the publication of this book, and I cannot thank them enough. I also appreciate Ankur Sumesra's timely assistance. My interactions with Sunanda Ghosh, Ashok R. Chandran, Sugata Ghosh and Meena Chakravorty of SAGE, in connection with this book, have been heartwarming.

I could not have completed this book without Ernest's love and support. His patience with me during my book writing phases deserves unlimited applause.

Premilla D'Cruz

Prologue

Creativity is critical for organizational progress and survival. This is even more so in the contemporary economic context where organizations today are facing a wider array of competitive pressures than ever before. Businesses believe that they cannot afford to do what they have always done. They must be constantly changing and innovating, reinventing themselves at internet speed to stay ahead of technological changes, new competitors around the globe and the continually shifting demands of customers and potential employees (DeGraff and Lawrence 2002). These complex demands have forced organizations to re-examine their style of functioning (Williams and Yang 1999). Organizations have no choice but to create value for their internal and external stakeholders and creativity is the key to this end. To remain competitive, businesses can no longer follow time-tested formulas. They must be able to produce and be receptive to creativity (Williams and Yang 1999). Indeed, as Khandwalla (2003) points out, contemporaneously, creativity is relevant to all aspects of organizational life including Human Resource Management (HRM) practices, growth strategies, marketing, operations and products, processes and services, taking the form of both technical and administrative innovations (Damanpour and Evan 1984; Hailey 2001). Creativity is thus moving beyond its traditional connotation of innovation of outstanding products and services to encompass the development of new processes, new ways of communicating with customers and new ways of attracting and retaining the best talent (DeGraff and Lawrence 2002).

Developing creativity as a core competence becomes imperative if organizations are to respond proactively to diverse pressures and maintain their competitive advantage. DeGraff and Lawrence (2002) maintain that creativity is the core of all competencies within an organization because it is the driving force behind anything that is better or new. The process of ensuring that creativity becomes a core competence at an organizational level is effectively captured by Teresa Amabile of Harvard Business School, who advocates the presence of three essential ingredients, namely, organizational motivation, resources and management practices (Amabile 1996a, 1996b).

Organizational motivation refers to the basic orientation of the organization towards creativity as well as supports for creativity throughout the organization. The orientation towards creativity must come from the highest levels of management, though lower levels are also important in communicating and interpreting that vision. The most important elements of the creativity orientation are value placed on creativity in general, an orientation towards risk (versus an orientation towards maintaining the status quo), a sense of pride in the organization's members and enthusiasm about what they are capable of doing, and an offensive strategy of taking the lead towards the future (versus a defensive strategy of simply wanting to protect the organization's past position). The primary organization-wide supports for creativity appear to be mechanisms for developing new ideas; open, active communication of information and ideas; reward and recognition for creative work; and fair evaluation of work (including work that might be perceived as a failure). Organizational motivation towards creativity includes the absence of several elements that can undermine creativity such as political problems, destructive criticism and competition within the organization, strict control by upper management, and an excess of formal structures and procedures (Amabile 1996a, 1996b).

Amabile (1996a, 1996b) cautions that organizational motivation alone is not enough. Organizations must engage all their resources to aid work in the domain targeted for creativity, including sufficient time for producing novel work in the domain, people with necessary expertise, funds allocated to this work domain, material resources, systems and processes for work in the domain, relevant information, and the availability of training.

Management practices at the level of the organization as a whole and at the level of individual departments and projects are critical. Creativity is fostered by allowing a considerable degree of freedom or autonomy in the conduct of one's work. The importance of a person-task fit cannot be undermined. In other words, individuals should be appropriately matched to work assignments on the basis of both skills and interests, to maximize a sense of positive challenge in the work.

Project supervision which encompasses an ability to clearly set overall project goals while allowing procedural autonomy, clear planning and feedback, good communication between the supervisor and the work group, and enthusiastic support for the work of individuals as well as the entire group, is vital. The constitution of effective work groups that represent a diversity of skills and are made up of individuals who trust and communicate well with each other, challenge each other's ideas in constructive ways, are mutually supportive, and are committed to the work they are doing, is crucial (Amabile 1996a, 1996b).

Developing a conducive organizational environment is a step in the right direction. But it is far from adequate. Since individuals form the basic unit of organizations, their ability to be creative is equally critical. In other words, the presence of an appropriate context promotes creativity only when there are people with creative thinking skills whose capabilities enable them to take advantage of and flourish in that context. Organizational success results from the convergence of the supportive organizational environment and the capable individual. To establish creativity as a core competence, then, organizations must go beyond merely developing an appropriate context and must staff themselves with creative people. But are there so many creative people around? The answer to this is complex.

That creative ability is universally present in all human beings is a widely held belief (Davis 1999; Guilford 1950; Nickerson 1999). Indeed, as with other cognitive abilities, the ability to be creative is present in all of us from the time of birth. Yet, the environment does little to develop these abilities. Exposure to social rules, traditions, expectations and conventions, pre-eminence accorded to convergent/logical thinking and emphasis on conformity stifle the excesses of early childhood generally characterized by uninhibited imagination and ideation, blocking creative abilities from developing further and from being expressed (Davis 1999; McCrae 1999). Research points out that by the time the child reaches Grade I/six years of age, he/she hardly demonstrates creative behavior (Epstein 1999). Indeed, though all of us are capable of a wide range of responses to life situations, we learn, in the process of growing up, that most of these are forbidden, and hence we restrict our responses to a narrow range of socially tolerated behaviors. While this has the advantage of making life predictable, since it is known what can be expected in everyday situations, the disadvantage is that unusual, unexpected reactions are discouraged and become rare (Cropley 1999). Instead of striking a balance between creative and convergent thinking, people cast aside their creative abilities as much as possible and live within the confines of logic and rationality.

Fortunately, this dismal state of affairs can be contained, if not reversed. Experts maintain that creativity can be developed and enhanced through two models, namely, the deficit model and the barrier model. The deficit model assumes that creative skills and abilities are not present in the individual's behavioral repertoire, and must be learned via instruction and training. Efforts made here target cognitive abilities and processes including ideation, problem redefinition and divergent thinking, and programs to inculcate, hone and internalize these skills are devised. At the end of the training, the individual acquires abilities and skills that were not previously present. The barrier model works on the assumption that the potential for creativity is inherently present in all of us but its development is inhibited by various blocks. Reinforcing facilitators and de-emphasizing blocks is the mandate of this approach. Procedures here, therefore, focus on attitudes, motivation, effort and so forth, and are targeted at sensitizing people to their own creativity and at removing inhibitors that prevent its manifestation. In addition, both models emphasize constructing environments that are conducive to the development and expression of creativity (Ripple 1999).

Creativity training programs have historically operated from the deficit standpoint, focusing on the cognitive abilities aspect of problem redefinition, ideation and divergent thinking. Yet, a complete training program that is truly interested in promoting creativity should embrace both the models, addressing all relevant components such as cognitive abilities, personality, motivation, effort, blocks, and so on (Lubart 1999; Ripple 1999). This book is in keeping with the second line of thinking. Providing instructors with a detailed program that covers creativity techniques, facilitators and inhibitors, the book is contextualized in the domain of management and hence is appropriate for participants employed in business organizations and for participants studying in business administration/management studies programs.

Part I of the book provides instructors with background reading material on creativity as a cognitive activity, influenced by facilitators and inhibitors. Armed with an understanding of creativity, instructors can move on to Part II of the book which contains the training component comprising five modules to be conducted over a span of five weeks. Systematic completion of Part II ensures the internalization of creative abilities by participants, together with greater sensitization to their own creative abilities, adoption of appropriate attitudes, self-efficacy, and reduction of blocks.

While creativity is now a core competence of the organization, the application of specific creativity techniques to real business situations must be conducted judiciously, keeping in mind the requirements of the situation and the decision making time available. High velocity occasions where there is limited time may call for problem redefinition, changing mindsets/schema, brainstorming, question banks and morphological analysis while comparatively slower paced occasions may permit longer drawn techniques such as random stimulation, force fitting triggers, componential detailing and fantasy trails. Nonetheless, the ability to engage creative ability at the workplace in a range of organizational functions will certainly contribute to organizational effectiveness and competitive advantage.

Part I

PART I

Understanding the Sphere of Creativity

DEFINING CREATIVITY

A lways associated with genius and breakthrough, creativity was earlier considered to be the privilege of a chosen few, beyond the reach of the majority of humankind. Placing creativity in the realm of the esoteric and the unattainable were mystical explanations which attributed it to divine intervention (Ripple 1999; Sternberg and Lubart 1999; Weisberg 2006). The creative person was seen as an empty vessel that a divine being would fill with inspiration. This not only meant that ideas originated outside the normal thinking process, but also that they originated outside the creative person, who merely served as a conduit through whom the ideas were presented from the Gods to the human race (Weisberg 2006). Creativity, thus, bore the mark of divine ancestry, fueling the notion that geniuses who unleash breakthroughs are born, not made (Ripple 1999).

Divine explanations of creativity were replaced by the theory of the unconscious in the psychoanalytic approach. Here, creativity was seen as arising from the tension between conscious reality and unconscious drives. Creativity was essentially a means of expressing unconscious wishes in a publicly acceptable fashion (Sternberg and Lubart 1999). At a conscious level, the creator remains oblivious to the role of and connection between unconscious ideas. Hence he/she is unable to pinpoint the source of and reasons for some of the ideas embodied in his/her work (Weisberg 2006).

The turning point in the conceptualization of creativity came with Guilford's historic 1950 presidential address to the American Psychological Association (Guilford 1950). Propounding the idea that creativity is not a gift from the Gods confined to eminent artists and scientists alone but is a cognitive ability demonstrated by all individuals, Guilford (1950) launched a new era in the understanding of creativity.

He replaced the earlier vague but intriguing notion of creativity with the distinct construct of divergent thinking (which implies the ability to produce many novel ideas), emphasizing its presence universally across humankind and providing direction for its measurement and development. His contribution not only firmly established creativity as a cognitive activity involving numerous mental structures and complex mental processes, but also underscored the view of creativity as a normative process available to everyone (Kurtzberg and Amabile 2000–2001; Ripple 1999). Moreover, thanks to Guilford's proposal that creativity could be measured via divergent thinking tasks capturing fluency, flexibility, originality and elaboration (Guilford 1950), a host of paper and pencil tests of creativity were spawned, introducing a psychometric dimension (Ripple 1999). Torrance Tests of Creative Thinking (Torrance 1974) remain the most notable among instruments developed to measure creative ability (Sternberg and Lubart 1999). Though the psychometric approach to creativity drew controversy in matters pertaining to reliability and validity (Sternberg and Lubart 1999), Guilford's (1950) idea that creativity could be developed through training and practice was widely espoused and resulted in the proliferation of instructional materials, procedures, techniques, and programs to improve creativity at home, in schools, and at the workplace (Ripple 1999).

As a cognitive activity, creativity engages a range of mental abilities and processes, such as remembering, imagining, planning, anticipating, judging, organizing, storing, deciding, determining, perceiving, comprehending, learning, recognizing and interpreting (Martinsen and Kaufmann 1999; Weisberg 2006), but its essential distinguishing features are problem redefinition and ideation. Redefining the problem provides the opportunity to look at a problem from different viewpoints, allowing diverse perspectives not immediately available to us to come to the fore. Ideation involves the generation of alternatives, triggered via the use of the imagination, associational thinking and other generative processes such as conceptual combination, analogical transfer, and so on. Problem redefinition and ideation allow novel and unique ideas to emerge. They are followed by evaluation which ensures the usefulness of the ideas.

The mental processes described above result in creative outcomes. While creative outcomes could be manifest as products, processes or thoughts, they are necessarily characterized by three dimensions: originality/uniqueness/novelty, appropriateness/relevance/effectiveness/ utility and ethics. Genuine creativity goes beyond mere novelty to respond appropriately to the issue at hand without causing harm (Cropley 1999; Khandwalla 2004). Outrageous ideas and non-conforming acts (Cropley 1999) as well as contrarian inclinations (Runco 1999a) that neither address the issue at stake nor serve the interests of society, are not defined as creative (Amabile and Tighe 1993; Cropley 1999; Runco 1999a). Creative outcomes must thus contribute a relevant and effective novelty that benefits society. As MacKinnon (1970) has indicated, the novelty of a product is not enough to justify its being called creative. Instead, the novel product must solve a problem and fit the needs of a given situation.

Creativity, then, is a complex phenomenon, encompassing both process and outcome. Drawing from and elaborating on the cognitive perspective outlined above, I define creativity as a cognitive activity falling in the realms of thinking, problem solving and information processing, that engages problem redefinition and ideation processes, followed by an evaluative component, to give rise to outcomes which are original, useful and ethical. As Khandwalla (2004) maintains, creativity is neither just the production of something novel and useful, because this could have occurred as a result of convergent cognitive activities, nor is it a mere mental process that sees linkages between unrelated ideas emerging from imagination and ideation, because if that was the case then dreaming would constitute creativity. On the contrary, creativity is the employment of a playfully exploratory rather than a mechanical process of problem solving, to find solutions that are novel and yet appropriate to the context (Khandwalla 2004).

A further viewpoint to the definition of creativity is propagated by Nickerson (1999) and Weisberg (2006) who submit that creativity can also be understood to mean original or novel for the individual involved, such that an entity would be considered creative if it is novel for the one who produces it, irrespective of how many others may have come up with it earlier. Thus, Nickerson (1999) states that one who rediscovers the Pythagorian theorem is being creative, despite the fact that the discovery is not new to the world. Similarly, Weisberg (2006) holds that a person who comes up with an idea for academic research in the course of reviewing literature only to later find that his/her idea has already been developed by someone else, is being creative because the idea is novel for him/her. The connotation of creativity being novelty/originality for the individual involved not only allows for creativity to be seen as an ability present in all human beings, but also permits each individual to be more creative, or less, in many aspects of daily life.

Creativity is alternatively termed as innovation and these nomenclatures are synonymous and interchangeable (Harvard Business School 2003; Van de Ven 1986; West and Rickards 1999), though some scholars distinguish innovation as being the successful implementation of creative ideas (Amabile 1996a; Khandwalla 2003; West and Rickards 1999).

LEVELS OF CREATIVITY

Guilford's (1950) view that creativity is a universal phenomenon has been endorsed by numerous experts who recognize that everyone can be creative, though not necessarily in the same way or to the same degree (Nickerson 1999). Evidence that all of us are capable of being creative becomes apparent when we are faced with new problems for which we have no ready solution and have to come up with one on our own.

Numerous typologies have been put forward to demonstrate the view that creativity is distributed across the population in varying degrees. Cropley (1999), for instance, distinguishes between the ordinary creativity of everyday life in which most people produce ideas or products that are new for them at their level and sublime creativity or the production of great works that are novel in the sense that they are widely hailed as enlarging human perspectives in some way not previously seen in history.

Gardner (1993) contrasts "little C creativity" which all of us evince in our daily lives through small departures in our daily routines with "big C creativity" which refers to breakthroughs which occur only very occasionally, shaping the ideas and standards of our culture.

Ripple (1999) discusses two classifications namely, the capital "C" versus small "c" typology and the psychological (P) versus historical (H) levels of creativity. Capital "C" creativity is a genius view which sees creativity as the special province of special individuals at rare moments in historical time. It involves bringing into existence something genuinely new that receives social validation and is valued enough to be added to culture. In contrast, small "c" creativity is specific to the individual, entailing ideas or products which are new to just that person. P creativity is conceptualized on the same lines as small "c" creativity, referring to ideas that are new to that person, irrespective of how many other people may have had that idea. H creativity refers to ideas that are new for the whole of human history (Ripple 1999).

In the case of sublime creativity/H creativity/capital "C" creativity, it is possible to distinguish between two levels: new applications of existing principles (secondary/minor creativity) and development of new principles (primary/major creativity). On the same lines, Ainsworth-Land (1982) proposes a continuum of four levels of creativity: (*i*) the base level which is merely an elaboration of an idea; (*ii*) the higher level which reflects an effort that results in an improvement; (*iii*) the still higher level which embodies a superior quality synthesis of previously unrelated ideas or perspectives or themes; and (*iv*) the highest level which depicts a genuine transformation that is revolutionary in its impact.

Sternberg et al. (2003) have developed the propulsion model of creative contributions which holds that creative contributions propel a field forward in some way. The propulsion model is a descriptive taxonomy of eight types of creative contributions. Each type may differ in the extent of creative contribution it makes, though there is no a priori way of evaluating the amount of creativity on the basis of the type of contribution. Sternberg et al. (2003) describe the eight types of creative contributions:

(1) Replication represents an effort to show that a given field is where it should be. The propulsion is intended to keep the field where it is rather than moving it.

(2) Redefinition refers to an attempt to redefine where the field currently is. The current status of the field thus is seen from a new point of view.

(3) Forward incrementation involves moving the field forward in the direction in which it is already proceeding, and the contribution takes the field to a point to which others are ready to go.

(4) Advance forward incrementation entails moving the field forward in the direction it is already going, but the contribution moves beyond where others are ready for the field to go.

(5) Redirection implies a move in the field from where it is currently headed towards a new and different direction.

(6) Reconstruction/redirection represents an endeavor to move the field back to where it once was (a reconstruction of the past) so that the field may move onward from that point in a direction different from the one it took in the past.

(7) Reinitiation marks an attempt to move the field to a different and as yet not reached starting point and then to move the field in a new direction from that point.

(8) Integration takes the field forward by putting together aspects of two or more past kinds of contributions that formerly were viewed as distinct or even opposed. This type of contribution shows particularly well the potentially dialectical nature of creative contributions in that it merges into a new Hegelian type of synthesis, two ideas that formerly may have been seen as opposed.

Goswami (1999) provides an interesting dimension to the debate, by highlighting the subjective component in the classification of creativity. According to him, classifications of creativity such as those described above ignore the subjective component, defining creativity only in terms of the field of external endeavor such as science, literature, art and music. Goswami (1999) asserts that these constitute outer creativity, that is, acts of creativity in the outer/objective arena. Personal transformation where a new context of being is discovered and is manifested into the personality of the creator is also an act of creation, which Goswami (1999) terms as inner creativity. Goswami (1999) cites the example of Mahatma Gandhi who not only made an impact on the culture of humankind through his discovery of the effectiveness of non-violence as a means of overcoming oppression but also his act of creation was intimately connected with his own personal transformation in that he became non-violent to the core. Given the pathbreaking contribution that personal transformation can make, Goswami (1999) asserts that the definition of an act of creation should be enlarged to include the subjective component of our own being as well.

CREATIVITY AS A COGNITIVE ACTIVITY

The essential distinguishing features of creativity as a cognitive activity emerge from two processes, viz., problem redefinition and ideation (see Figure I.1). Though problem redefinition ideally precedes ideation, quite often, people attempt to ideate without redefining. Sometimes, the relationship between the two could be characterized by iteration, where one starts with redefining and then moves on to ideation. If the emergent ideas do not lead towards a solution, one may return to redefining and follow it up with ideation.

Redefining the problem provides the opportunity to look at the situation from different viewpoints, allowing diverse perspectives not immediately available to us, to come to the fore. Generally, the initial way in which one looks at a problem is biased by past experience, learning, knowledge and habit, and redefinition permits alternative points of view to emerge, often leading to a holistic understanding. Redefinition takes place by looking at a problem from one perspective and then moving on to another perspective and then to still another. With each move, the understanding deepens and one begins to comprehend the essence of the problem. In this way, one not only breaks out of the confines of existing thought processes that are limiting but one also grasps the multiple and complex dimensions of the problem (Proctor 1999). This exercise, by itself, may help us solve the problem. If it does not do that, the process of redefinition any way gives a direction to the process of solution generation by providing newer/different approaches to the problem.

Figure I.1   *Creativity as a Cognitive Activity*

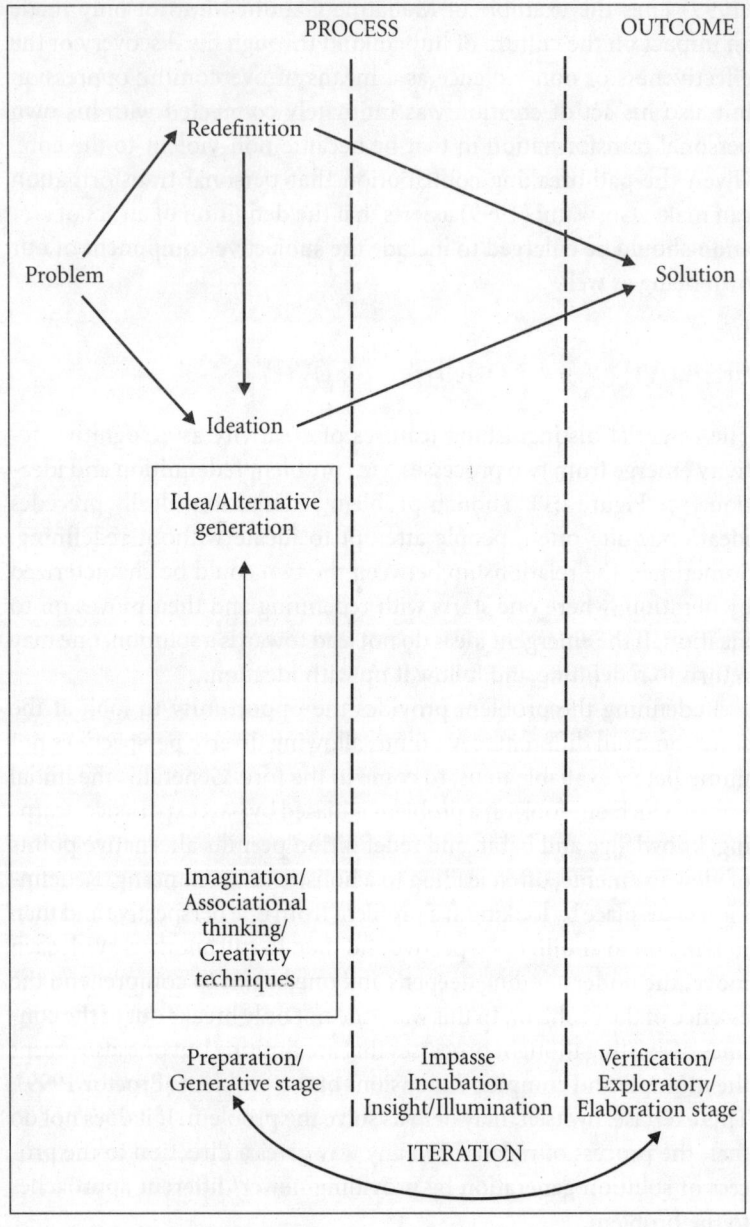

PROCESS   OUTCOME

Redefinition

Problem   Solution

Ideation

Idea/Alternative
generation

Imagination/
Associational
thinking/
Creativity
techniques

Preparation/	Impasse	Verification/
Generative stage	Incubation	Exploratory/
	Insight/Illumination	Elaboration stage

ITERATION

Ideation involves the generation of alternatives, triggered via the use of the imagination (Singer 1999) and/or of associational thinking (Koestler 1964; Mednick 1962; Rothenberg 1999a, 1999b; Ward et al. 1999) and/or other generative processes (Ward et al. 1999). All of us are born with the ability to ideate but this often gets stifled during the process of socialization. Recharging, developing and maintaining the ability to ideate is possible through training in and practice with creativity techniques. Undoubtedly, ideas could vary in their novelty/uniqueness on a continuum from slightly original to highly original.

Imagination is a special feature or form of human thought characterized by the ability of the individual to reproduce images or concepts originally derived from the basic senses but now reflected in one's consciousness as memories, fantasies, or future plans. These sensory derived images can be reshaped and recombined into new images or possible future dialogues that may range from regretful ruminations about the past to rehearsals or practical planning for future anticipated events, and in some cases, to the production of creative works of art, literature or science (Singer 1999). When ideating for creativity, the imagination is encouraged to freewheel or run wild without censorship or judgment so that whatever ideas come up are retained. These ideas could be used as stimuli to develop solutions or to generate more ideas for solutions in an associational thinking process.

Associational thinking, rooted in the proposition that the mind consists entirely of ideas (words, images, formulas, and so on), each of which is associated with other ideas (Dacey 1999), is the process of linking ideas (Cropley 1999). It involves moving from one idea to another by way of a chain of associations (Dacey 1999). Suggestions for associational thinking have been put forward by numerous experts.

Mednick (1962), for example, has put forward the theory of associative hierarchies. According to him, in the course of their experiences, people learn a number of responses to a particular stimulus. These stimulus-response associations (or pairings) are developed into a hierarchy, depending on the frequency of their occurrence. Associations that occur frequently stand higher in the hierarchy with a higher probability of being selected when the stimulus recurs as compared to associations that occur infrequently. The less-likely associations are "remote" and people who make them produce unusual and unexpected ideas (Cropley 1999). Individuals with steep gradients in their hierarchy of associations tend to give more common associations and few uncommon associations while those with flat gradients give more uncommon associations and few common associations (Fasko 1999). Mednick (1962) underscored that creative individuals exhibited flat gradients in their associative hierarchies in contrast to less creative individuals whose gradients were steep. He further suggested that individuals who develop large numbers of associations for a problem have a higher probability of coming up with a creative solution. Thus, people with restricted hierarchies, in which there are one or two dominant responses, do not tend to think creatively. This is so because these responses, which occur often and quickly, block the production of less-frequent responses, resulting in stereotyped and familiar responses being made to a situation. Such people end up being at a disadvantage when novel responses (that is, relatively infrequent responses) are demanded. Creative individuals, in contrast, possess expanded associative hierarchies in which a relatively large number of responses, of more or less equal probability, are available. Such individuals have a much greater likelihood of coming up with a relatively unusual response to a situation, which could result in a creative outcome (Weisberg 2006). Mednick (1962: 221), thus, defines the creative thinking process as "the forming of associative elements into new combinations which either meet specified requirements or are in some way useful. The more mutually remote the elements of the new combination, the more creative the process or solution".

Koestler (1964) developed the concept of bisociation which involves combining two completely unrelated entities such that the linkage sparks off unusual ideas that result in creative breakthroughs. Koestler (1964) constrasts this with association where related entities are linked and the ideas so emerging remain within the realm of the known and the usual. According to bisociation, ideas occur in matrices or fields. Normally, ideas from the same field are combined in a process of association. However, some people combine ideas from separate matrices in a process of bisociation, which by virtue of the fact that the ideas are not normally found together, means that the combination is surprising (Cropley 1999). Koestler (1964) believes that in order for connections to be established via bisociation, unconscious processing is critical because this facilitates insights that break away from the confines of logic and habit. Association, on the other hand, being rooted in logic and habit, operates via conscious cognitive processes and hence does not lead to breakthroughs in thinking. Koestler (1964) cites the example of Guttenberg's invention of the printing press with movable type. Guttenberg's idea resulted from his visit to a wine festival where he realized that the press used to crush grapes could be used to apply type to paper. Thus, the movable-type printing press was born.

Rothenberg (1999a, 1999b) suggests homospatial and janusian processes as means of developing associations. The homospatial process consists of actively conceiving two or more discrete identities occupying the same space, a conception leading to the articulation of new identities. In this process, concrete entities such as rivers, houses, rockets, animals and human faces as well as sensory data such as sound patterns, visual images, tactile sensations and written words are brought together in the mind such that they totally fill its perceptual space, stimulating, as a result, unusual ideas (Rothenberg 1999a). He elaborates via an example. A poet produced the metaphor "the branches were handles of stars" through a homospatial process where the shared sound qualities and the shared shapes of the wooden objects "branch" and "handle" led him to believe that they ought to be together and hence he superimposed them in his mind. As the poet experienced a vivid impression of the letter "a" overlapping in the two words, the idea of stars was generated, and the metaphor was created (Rothenberg 1999a).

The janusian process, derived from the qualities of the Roman god, Janus, who had faces that looked in multiple, diametrically opposite directions simultaneously, consists of actively yet concomitantly conceiving multiple opposites or antitheses. During the course of the creative process, opposite or antithetical ideas, concepts, or propositions are consciously conceptualized as simultaneously coexisting. Although seemingly illogical and self-contradictory, these formulations are constructed in clearly logical and rational states of mind to produce creative effects. They occur as early conceptions in the development of scientific theories and artworks and at critical junctures at middle and later stages as well. Because they serve generative functions during both formative and critical stages of the creative process, these simultaneous antitheses or opposites usually undergo transformation and modification and are seldom directly discernible in final created products. They are formulated by the creative thinker as solutions in working out practical and scientific tasks and as central ideas for artwork (Rothenberg 1999b).

Other generative processes include the retrieval of existing structures from memory, the formation of simple associations among those structures or combinations of them, the mental synthesis of new structures, the mental transformation of existing structures into new forms, conceptual combination and expansion/extension, analogical transfer of information from one domain to another, and categorical reduction in which existing structures are conceptually reduced to more primitive constituents (Ward et al. 1999).

Both problem redefinition and ideation abilities can be developed, enhanced, and internalized through training and practice with creativity techniques such as brainstorming, morphological analysis, lateral thinking and synectics, and their variants.

Problem redefinition and ideation are aligned with divergent thinking, that is, the ability to find substantial numbers of new, original and unexpected answers, generally to loosely defined problems for which there is no prior correct solution (Guilford 1950), and this is characterized as imaginative, uninhibited, inventive, unpredictable and revolutionary (Nickerson 1999), with the quality of the output being judged from the perspectives of Guilford's (1950) principles of fluency, flexibility and originality.

Fluency refers to the number of ideas that a person is able to come up with in order to solve a given problem. The more ideas a person can generate, the more ideationally fluent he/she is. For example, if a group of people are asked to list the number of uses a coaster can serve, those listing a higher number will be considered to be more ideationally fluent than those listing a smaller number.

Flexibility takes into account the range of themes or categories encompassed by the ideas generated. The greater the range of themes or categories covered, the higher the flexibility demonstrated. In the instance of coasters referred to above, the person providing five uses of coasters as a dining/beverage device exemplifies the absence of flexibility in contrast to the flexibility shown by the person whose five uses of coasters include a wall-hanging, a bookmark, a fashion accessory, a tool for sports and games and a lampshade.

Originality emphasizes the ability to come up with unusual, unique, novel and innovative ideas as potential solutions to a given problem. In the case of coasters, their use as earrings or knee pads may be considered unusual, and therefore, original responses. A related ability is the ability to come up with novel relationships between ideas.

For problem redefinition and ideation to be effective, suspension of judgment/evaluation is mandatory. This is so because it is only by withholding judgment/evaluation that a free and uninhibited generation and flow of wild and remote ideas is facilitated. As a result, a greater number of and more unusual and unique ideas emerge and are retained. This not only increases the pool from which potential solutions can be drawn but also serves as stimulation for breeding further ideas.

The processes of problem redefinition and ideation described above correspond with the generative phase of Finke et al.'s (1992) geneplore model and with the preparation phase of Wallas's (1926) stage model (see Figure I.1).

As mentioned earlier, problem redefinition and/or ideation provide potential solutions for the problem situation. The initial ideas generated during this time are sometimes described as pre-inventive in the sense that they are not complete but rather may be an untested proposal or even a mere germ of an idea, but they hold some promise of responding to the situation at hand (Ward et al. 1999). In other words, initial ideas could be wild/remote and impractical/unfeasible. They need to be followed up with the exploratory (Finke et al. 1992) or verification (Wallas 1926) stage, characterized essentially by convergent thinking in which alternatives are evaluated and appropriately developed to meet the demands of the problem situation (see Figure I.1). Convergent thinking which includes categorization, logical thinking, analysis, comparison, evaluation, and so on (Khandwalla 2004), is associated with well-defined, structured problems which have prior correct solutions (Ripple 1999). Convergent thinking emphasizes logic, reality, practicality, conservatism and dependability (Nickerson 1999) and can be regarded as the mental abilities that facilitate the assessment and elaboration of an innovative solution (Khandwalla 2004).

Guilford (1950) considers elaboration to be the key principle during the exploratory/verification stage. According to him, elaboration, which is indispensable in putting a creative idea to work, comprises the ability to add detail and depth to complete an idea and has also been recognized as a significant creative ability. Csikszentmihalyi and Sawyer (1995) provide evidence for the verification/exploratory stage. They state that after an idea is reached, it needs to be shaped and evaluated to fit reality, a process they term elaboration.

The transition from the generative/preparation stage to the exploratory/verification/elaboration stage need not proceed smoothly. In other words, it is possible that the ideas generated via problem redefinition and ideation do not lend themselves to appropriate and useful solutions and hence a return to the generative/preparatory stage becomes inevitable. In this manner, iteration between the preparation/generative and exploratory/verification/elaboration stages continues until a solution is finalized (see Figure I.1).

It is important to recognize that even the iterative process between the preparation/generative and the exploratory/verification/elaboration stages may not be immediately successful in finding a solution to the problem. Instead, it may face an impasse during which awareness of and movement towards a potential solution are blocked despite extensive problem redefinition and ideation. The resolution of an impasse involves a time lapse since it occurs after an incubation period during which the problem is temporarily put aside. Illumination/insight, which is the sudden realization of a solution that occurs either during time away from the problem, or when one returns to the problem after the incubation period, breaks the impasse and ends the incubation period (Smith and Dodds 1999). Impasse, incubation and illumination as described here parallel Wallas's (1926) incubation and insight/illumination phases, though some experts (Weisberg 2006) doubt Wallas's (1926) emphasis on the role of the unconscious during these phases (see Figure I.1).

Three sets of viewpoints are put forward to explain incubation and insight/illumination: the role of unconscious processing, critiques of and alternatives to the unconscious processing thesis, and the gestalt school.

Proponents of the unconscious processing perspective define illumination/insight (also known as the A-ha experience) as the sudden appearance in one's consciousness of a creative idea or solution to a problem when one had not been thinking about the matter consciously. That the insight emerges when one is not consciously thinking about this problem, is taken as evidence of unconscious processing. Incubation, which involves thinking about the problem unconsciously while one is consciously thinking about something else, is forwarded as the explanation for sudden illumination (Weisberg 2006).

Psychological theorizing about creative thinking from the unconscious perspective draws on the pioneering work of Poincare which has been adapted and honed by numerous researchers (Weisberg 2006) including Wallas (1926), Csikszentmihalyi (1996) and Csikszentmihalyi and Sawyer (1995) whose views are included here. Poincare (in Weisberg 2006) maintains that illumination/insight occurs when one is engaged in something else, that is, when one is not consciously engaged with the problem at hand. It is believed that illumination occurs because one is thinking about the problem at an unconscious level. In other words, unconscious work is critical for creative thinking, and illumination is the result of long, unconscious prior work. Yet illumination/insight generally occurs without warning or presence of any external stimulus (Csikszentmihalyi and Sawyer 1995).

The unconscious operates by building combinations of ideas. Creativity is the discovery of valuable combinations of ideas. The unconscious helps by combining ideas that, because of their remoteness from each other, are not considered consciously because they are not seen as being related to each other (Poincare, in Weisberg 2006). Conscious thought produces ideas in a linear, logical manner, whereas during incubation, ideas churn below the threshold of consciousness. Unconscious processing allows for random combinations of ideas that go beyond the bounds of strict logic so that unusual connections may be made—the unconscious succeeds in producing combinations of ideas that are not possible in conscious processing (Csikszentmihalyi 1996).

But the unconscious is also discerning, being able to avoid useless/ sterile combinations that emerge from the linkage of disparate ideas. This discernment is triggered by the earlier conscious work (both work undertaken during the preparation phase and prior knowledge/ expertise of the domain) which influences unconscious processing because it filters the combinatorial process so that those ideas that have some chance (even a remote one) of making a worthwhile contribution are selected for further processing. Through the unconscious combinatorial process which operates in conjunction with previous conscious work, a potentially useful combination is hit upon and bursts suddenly into consciousness where it is experienced as illumination/ insight (Poincare, in Weisberg 2006).

An idea moves from unconsciousness to consciousness when the unconscious sensitivity of the thinker evaluates it as either being the correct one or having the potential to lead to the correct one. This unconscious thus has a gatekeeping mechanism which ensures that we remain oblivious to sterile/unpromising combinations whose properties fail the unconscious's evaluation criteria, thereby being unable to get past the gatekeeper into consciousness (Poincare, in Weisberg 2006).

The leap from incubation to insight displays large individual differences, taking years in some cases and hours in others. In other words, the time frame for insight processes varies from short term to long term. Csikszentmihalyi and Sawyer (1995) propose that these differences in the time frame of insight processes arise essentially due to the nature of the problem being dealt with. Problems that call for revolutionary paradigm shifts rather than incremental normal science changes (Kuhn 1962) often entail long time-frame insight processes (Csikszentmihalyi and Sawyer 1995).

Unconscious processing is believed to have a greater capacity than conscious processing. Conscious processing is a serial processor with limited capacity while unconscious processing is a parallel processor that works simultaneously on multiple problems. How individuals direct unconscious processes to make useful insights is not known (Csikszentmihalyi and Sawyer 1995).

Weisberg (2006) questions the evidence put forth to support the unconscious processing thesis. Pointing out that the empirical support for the role of unconscious processing in creativity comes from anecdotal reports which do not constitute adequate grounds on which to build a scientific theory, he goes on to state that modern evidence for unconscious processing is no stronger than that brought forth by Poincare a century ago. He further proposes alternative explanations such as selective forgetting and opportunistic assimilation to account for creative insights/illumination.

Let us first look at the issue of selective forgetting. When a problem is not solved as a result of the initial attempts, those attempts could be in the wrong direction. Yet the ideas underlying those attempts linger in our minds, causing a fixation/mental rut, such that immediate later attempts remain within the ambit of the earlier ideas and hence they also turn out to be unsuccessful. Taking a break, such as an incubation period, allows for the ideas suggested by the unsuccessful approaches to be forgotten, making space for new ideas to replace them and direct the problem solving endeavor (Smith 1995).

Opportunistic assimilation has been propounded by Seifert et al. (1995). According to them, when a break is taken after reaching an impasse in problem solving, the unsolved problem remains stored in memory as a failure index, making it a unique type of memory. Failure indices specify the general type of information needed to solve the problem, that is, the problem is stored as containing a gap, along with a general description of the type of information that might fill that gap. When the individual encounters an environmental or mental event that matches the information required to solve the problem, the problem is retrieved, and the thinker experiences illumination/insight. Seifert et al. (1995) term this an "opportunistic assimilation" because by assimilating relevant events that he or she happens to encounter, the individual is opportunistic in taking advantage of his or her experiences. They maintain that unconscious processing does not play a role in problem solving. Rather, a break may help problem solving because during this time, an accidental encounter with an event may provide the relevant solution.

Gestalt psychologists, the third group attempting to explain insight/ illumination and incubation, employ the lens of perception rather than unconscious processing. According to them, insight/illumination, which occurs after an impasse, provides a solution to the problem at hand via restructuring, which involves a new way of perceiving and approaching the problem. Impasses arise essentially because of the restrictive interference of past experience. That is, we tend to rely excessively on the past to understand and respond to problems that we encounter (a phenomenon termed as fixation), but unfortunately past experience and habitual modes of problem solving do not always lend themselves to new situations, resulting in impasses. Stated differently, fixation with the past could lead to a structuring of the problem such that finding a solution is hampered. In the Gestalt view, the basic mechanism underlying insight/illumination and moving out of the impasse is the person's ability to discover an alternate structure of the problem, achieved by breaking away from the confines of past experience. No specialized knowledge is needed to break out of an impasse and achieve insight into a problem situation (Weisberg 2006).

Whereas earlier proponents of the Gestalt school held that restructuring occurred spontaneously, the contemporary view is that heuristics influence the restructuring process. Ohlsson (1992) suggests three of these, namely, elaboration (finding a different way to describe an object or objects in the problem), recoding (including some previously ignored object in the problem), and relaxation of goal constraints (changing the goals of the problem or the methods to be used in reaching the goals).

Depending on the complexity of the problem, restructuring can bring about complete or partial insight. If a problem situation is relatively simple, restructuring may result in the complete solution becoming immediately available. On the other hand, if a problem situation is relatively complex, then a restructuring may result only in the thinker's seeing a new solution path or direction, but not the complete solution (Weisberg 2006).

It is the Gestalt view which has led to a widespread belief that productive problem solving, as well as creative thinking in general, comes about only by breaking away from experience and letting our ideas roam freely. The exhortation to think outside the box in order to be productive and creative is a direct influence of the Gestalt school (Weisberg 2006).

Once the impasse is resolved, and potential solutions are identified, Wallas's (1926) verification or Finke et al.'s (1992) exploratory stage follows (see Figure I.1). That creativity calls for both divergent and convergent thinking underscores that these two processes are complementary, not antagonistic. While it was earlier believed that divergent and convergent thinking were polar opposites such that an engagement with one implied a move away from the other, the contemporary view asserts that both divergent and convergent dimensions color an individual's thinking and are equally important for problem solving (Nickerson 1999). Divergent thinking is useful for generating ideas while convergent thinking is useful for developing them further. In other words, while divergent thinking enhances the effectiveness of convergent thinking by offering more ideas to select from, convergent thinking accentuates the value of divergent thinking by making good use of the ideas generated (De Bono 1990). Undoubtedly, divergent and convergent abilities are both required in order to think effectively. To summarize in Nickerson's (1999) words, divergent thinking, at its best, generates original ideas, unusual approaches to problems and novel perspectives in terms of which to view situations while convergent thinking evaluates what divergent thinking offers, subjects the possibilities to criteria of acceptability, and selects some from among them for further consideration.

As Figure I.1 highlights, creativity encompasses both process and outcome dimensions. Not only is the outcome/solution unique and novel but the process by which one arrived at it also includes problem redefinition and ideation, engaging divergent thinking abilities.

It may be relevant to highlight that creativity lends itself to the resolution of all kinds of problems. While problems vary in terms of their definition, the availability of means to solve them and the clarity of the criteria for recognizing solutions, creativity is traditionally associated with non-routine or ill-defined problems which require, in the first instance, becoming aware that there is a problem at all and finding a way of defining it; second, working out techniques for solving the problem; and third, development of criteria for recognizing a solution. Such "complex" or "intractable" problems do not lend themselves to a habitual mode of problem solving, but instead, demand a high level of creativity (Cropley 1999; Mayer 1999). In contrast, clearly defined/routine problems which are solvable by means of standard techniques and which have obvious and well-known criteria for identifying solutions (Cropley 1999; Mayer 1999), are generally solved without the help of creativity, that is, we solve them in a habitual manner, relying on cognitive mechanisms and processes that we have used in the past (Mayer 1999). Yet it is important to recognize that even in these instances, though we are successful in solving the problem, it may be beneficial to explore alternatives which may provide better and more effective solutions. Creativity can thus be brought into play here too. Clearly, the opportunity to be creative is perennial, presenting itself in every facet of an individual's life through both familiar and unfamiliar experiences.

THE DEVELOPMENT AND MANIFESTATION OF CREATIVITY

Guilford (1950) stated that while each of us has the ability to be creative, the manifestation of creative ability is contingent on many variables. These can be broadly classified into two perspectives. One view maintains that creativity arises as a consequence of facilitating factors while the other stand claims that the absence of inhibitory factors allows for creativity to be expressed.

The facilitator approach

The factors facilitating creativity can be divided into two tiers comprising primary level factors and secondary level factors. Primary level factors (tier 1) include motivation, effort and self-efficacy while secondary level factors (tier 2) include personality, environment and training. Primary level factors together are critical for creative thinking: in their absence, creative thinking will not be possible. Primary level factors subsume secondary level factors whose contribution is indirect: that is, secondary level factors are necessary conditions for creative thinking, but their presence is insufficient, and therefore ineffective, without primary level factors (see Figure I.2).

Primary level factors

Motivation

Motivation is of primary significance in the development of creativity. That is, the individual should desire to become creative. In the absence of a desire to think divergently, take risks, defy conventional opinion, or expose oneself to the possibility of being wrong, creative expression is unlikely. Purpose, in other words, an abiding intention to develop one's creative potential, is critical. Strong motivation, therefore, provides the basis for the development of creative potential (Nickerson 1999).

Figure 1.2   **Two-tier Model of Factors Facilitating Creative Thinking**

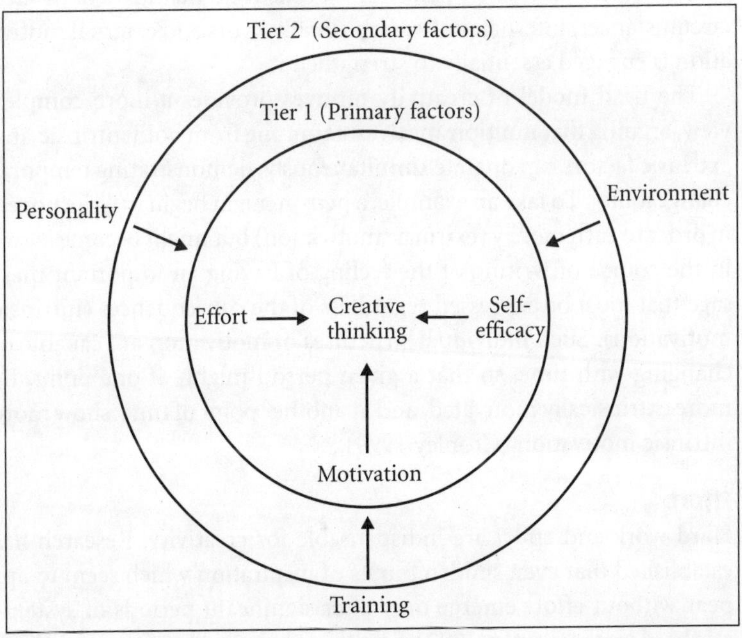

Creativity researchers generally agree that not only is motivation essential to creativity, but also that internal, or intrinsic motivation (that is, the wish to carry out an activity for the sake of the activity itself) is a more effective determinant of creativity than is external, or extrinsic, motivation (that is, the hope of obtaining external rewards)

(see, for example, Amabile 1983, 1996a, 1996b; Hennessey and Amabile 1988; Plucker and Runco 1999). Some claim that external motivation can actually undermine creativity because of the manner in which it can lead people to work in directions that provide external rewards, such as personal recognition by peers, colleagues or superiors, praise, promotion, or fame (Cropley 1999). In such cases, the person is motivated by the external rewards rather than by the creative goal.

While the roles of internal and external motivation in creativity continue to be debated (Plucker and Runco 1999), Nickerson (1999) suggests that external motivators can be used as a means of reinforcing internal motivation and encouraging the expression of natural abilities such that creative behavior is evoked and maintained. In such circumstances, internal motivation already exists and external motivation is engaged essentially to strengthen it.

The triad model of creativity motives provides a more complex view, arguing that multiple motives stemming from both intrinsic and extrinsic factors can operate simultaneously, demonstrating temporal changeability. To take an example, a person might begin to write novels in order to earn money (extrinsic motivation) but might become aware in the course of writing of the feeling of having an important message that must be expressed regardless of the consequences (intrinsic motivation). Such individual structures of motivation are capable of changing with time, so that a given person might, at one point, be more extrinsically motivated, and at another point of time, show more intrinsic motivation (Cropley 1999).

Effort

Hard work and effort are indispensable for creativity. Research has established that even sudden bursts of inspiration which seem to appear without effort emerge only after significant periods of systematic hard work (Cropley 1999). So although there are reasons to believe that modest efforts would probably suffice to increase the degree of creativity most of us exhibit in our daily lives, truly outstanding creative works in science and art have often taken many years to produce (Nickerson 1999).

Effort involves a command over the area/domain in which one is seeking to be creative. Undoubtedly, knowledge of a domain does not

always lead to creativity, but such knowledge does appear to be a relatively necessary condition for it; people who do noteworthy creative work
in any given domain are almost invariably very knowledgeable about
the domain (Cropley 1999; Plucker and Runco 1999). This is so because
creative solutions emerge from the reworking of existing knowledge,
and so before one can reasonably hope to change a domain, one must
master the domain as it exists (Cropley 1999; Csikszentmihalyi 1996).
There is, however, a caveat. Very high levels of domain-specific
knowledge can, in some instances, work against creativity (Plucker and
Runco 1999) because experts in that area can become so committed
to a particular way of approaching problems that they become reluc-
tant to consider alternative approaches (Frensch and Sternberg 1989;
Plucker and Runco 1999; Simonton 1984). Knowledge can sometimes
produce a constraining tunnel-vision. In such instances, openness and
flexibility provide the necessary balance (Cropley 1999).

Self-efficacy
Motivation should necessarily be coupled with self-efficacy, that is,
the belief that one can be creative. One's belief in his/her ability to be
creative forms the psychological foundation of creative achievement
(Plucker and Runco 1999). It is hard to imagine a belief that is more
important to creativity than the belief that how one's mind is developed
and used is one's personal responsibility (Nickerson 1999). Believing that
one can become creative through training and practice, supported by
appropriate influences, rather than being solely genetically determined,
motivates effort which in turn promotes self-realization.

Secondary level factors

Personality
Recognizing the role of personality in creativity, there is considerable research focusing on the identification of personality characteristics that distinguish more creative persons from those who are less
creative (Nickerson 1999). Davis (1999), for instance, has identified
15 categories of positive, desirable traits that promote creative thinking including awareness of and appreciation for creativity, originality,
independence and confidence, risk-taking ability and resourcefulness,

energy and intrinsic motivation, curiosity, sense of humor, attraction to complexity and ambiguity, capacity for fantasy, artistic and sensitive nature, open-mindedness and flexibility, reflective and introspective orientation, intuition and perception, emotionality and ethics.

Proctor (1999) points out that a creative person is one who challenges the status quo, exhibits curiosity, investigates new possibilities, shows initiative, is highly imaginative, harbors no fear of taking risks, demonstrates willingness to make mistakes, adapts to different kinds of environments, copes with paradoxes and ambiguities, looks beyond the first right idea, sees possibilities in the seemingly impossible, and discerns relationships between seemingly disconnected elements.

Cropley (1999) highlights the complexity of the relationship between creativity and personality. According to him, creativity calls for a complex personality that combines, among others, sensitivity with toughness or high intelligence with naiveté. In other words, the personality characteristics regarded as important for creativity sometimes seem to be contradictory: for instance, the creative personality seems to be simultaneously stereotypically masculine (independence, self-confidence, risk-taking ability) and yet stereotypically feminine (sensitivity, intuition, emotionality). Creativity requires possession of a paradoxical personality characterized by several polarities: openness combined with a drive to close incomplete gestalts; acceptance of fantasy combined with maintenance of a strong sense of reality; critical and destructive attitudes together with constructive problem solving; cool neutrality combined with passionate engagement; self-centeredness co-existing with altruism; self-criticism and self-doubt together with self-confidence; and tension and concentration side by side with relaxedness.

While Khandwalla (2004) advocates self-awareness and desire to change as critical prerequisites for acquiring appropriate traits and shedding inappropriate ones, the issue of whether the relationship between creativity and personality is correlational or causative is unclear. Apart from that, another issue that calls for clarity is the extent to which relevant personality traits are determined by genetic factors or shaped by environmental circumstances (Nickerson 1999). The available evidence indicates the role of both factors though the precise contribution of each has not yet been measured.

Environment

Developing a creativogenic environment (that is, an environment conducive to creative thinking [Arieti 1976]) involves focusing on numerous dimensions. Apart from the presence of sufficient and appropriate material and financial resources and time, a stimulating environment which promotes curiosity, exploration, challenge, new experiences, complexity, coupled with constructive and well-timed feedback and criticism, appropriate reinforcement, tolerance for experimentation and risk-taking, and learning from blocks and failures, is ideal (Khandwalla 2004; Plucker and Runco 1999). Social networks where significant others such as parents, teachers, and peers hold norms favoring creativity, and communicate expectations to the individual of a creative effort by the latter, stimulates creativity. An environment in which admired high-status persons hold anti-innovation norms or are indifferent to creativity, or fail to communicate their expectation of creative effort to the individual, or communicate the expectation of a conformist response, discourages creativity (Khandwalla 2004; Plucker and Runco 1999).

Creativity is associated with curiosity and exploration that involve a persistent reluctance to take things for granted, a skepticism of accepted explanations and a desire to go beyond the obvious. The ability to see things from different perspectives and the willingness and ability to change one's perspective have been stressed by many investigators as important aspects of creative thinking. The emphasis is on curiosity as an abiding orientation that determines one's lifestyle (Nickerson 1999; Plucker and Runco 1999).

We are all born with a natural sense of curiosity. Yet whether we maintain this orientation through the course of our lives depends on the extent to which it is encouraged or inhibited during our formative years. Generally, early agents of socialization, in particular the education process, stifle our curiosity by rebuffing our inquisitiveness and routinely providing "just because" answers to our "why" questions, ensuring as a result that we become less interested in exploring the mysteries of our existence. The idea that children are naturally curious and that early educational experiences stymie their curiosity is a very disturbing one. Determining the extent to which specific educational practices stifle creativity is an area that deserves much attention (Nickerson 1999).

Notwithstanding the dampening effect of our external environment, we can stimulate our own curiosity by being attentive and observant, questioning our experiences, re-examining ideas that we take for granted, and delving further into the world around us. Indeed, it is through the process of exploration that we become aware of our preferences and find avenues that genuinely interest us. Working in areas that hold our attention sparks off internal motivation, so critical for the development of our creative potential (Nickerson 1999).

To quote Csikszentmihalyi (1996: 11):

> Each of us is born with two contradictory sets of instructions: a conservative tendency, made up of instincts for self-preservation, self-aggrandizement, and saving energy, and an expansive tendency made up of instincts for exploring, for enjoying novelty and risk—the curiosity that leads to creativity belongs to this set. We need both of these programs. But whereas the first tendency requires little encouragement or support from outside to motivate behavior, the second can wilt if it is not cultivated. If too few opportunities for curiosity are available, if too many obstacles are placed in the way of risk and exploration, the motivation to engage in creative behavior is easily extinguished.

Training in creative thinking skills

Though creative ability is universal across humankind, social influences hamper its development and expression. There is sufficient evidence to support the belief that training and practice rekindle, develop and maintain creative thinking (Amabile 1983; Amabile and Tighe 1993; Cropley 1992; Finke et al. 1992; Plucker and Runco 1999; Ripple 1999; Sternberg and Lubart 1996). Indeed, the deficit approach to improving creativity emphasizes that training and instruction are instrumental in adding creativity skills to the individual's behavioral repertoire (Ripple 1999). Nickerson (1999), Plucker and Runco (1999) and Ripple (1999) document numerous programs and approaches based on techniques such as problem restructuring, morphological analysis, checklists, attribute listing, synectics, lateral thinking, and brainstorming to illustrate that training is resorted to in enhancing creativity. Indeed, repeated and prolonged engagement with these techniques results in their internalization so that creative thinking becomes a habit. At the same time, it is important to acknowledge that while training and practice will undoubtedly enhance an individual's creative thinking ability, inter-individual differences will persist.

While recognizing the role of the aforementioned factors, a balanced approach is indispensable. That is, though it is important to be able to engage in creative expression without fear of ridicule or reprimand, it does not mean that in the interest of not stifling creativity, people should be allowed to do whatever they wish. Although creativity can be stifled by a repressive environment, it is not necessarily fostered by total lack of constraint. Too little structure can be as inhibiting of creativity as too much. The need for structure, discipline, self-restraint, and respect for tradition and convention is as real and important as the need for freedom, spontaneity, innovativeness, and risk taking (Nickerson 1999). It is an environment that provides freedom of thought and action but equally demands responsibility, accountability, and effective performance, that encourages creativity. Both freedom without responsibility and an authoritarian environment are equally destructive of creativity (Khandwalla 2004). While risk-taking should be encouraged, irresponsible and dangerous risks should be discouraged. The critical issue is to manage risks rather than to take any risk that presents itself (Plucker and Runco 1999). The challenge is to find the proper balance between recognizing and respecting rules, bounds, and limits without stifling creativity. This means teaching not only what rules are, but also why rules are necessary and why particular rules make sense (Nickerson 1999). In other words, creative discretion must be cultivated (Plucker and Runco 1999).

Finding the right balance between demand and support is also a challenge. While it is necessary to have goals that stretch capabilities, it is also necessary to have a supportive environment that rewards effort even when it is not successful. There is a reason to believe that environments that are both demanding and supportive are more conducive to the development of creativity than those that have much of one of these characteristics but little of the other (Nickerson 1999).

The inhibitor approach

The inhibitor approach to creativity assumes that while the potential for creativity is inherent in all individuals, various blocks such as cultural blocks, cognitive blocks, emotional blocks, and resource blocks inhibit its development and manifestation. Creative expression occurs when these inhibitory factors are removed, sensitizing people to their own creative thinking ability (Proctor 1999; Ripple 1999).

Cultural blocks

Cultural blocks arise essentially from the pressures to conform to and comply with social norms. Through formal and informal socialization processes and influences, we learn culturally accepted ways of life, internalizing "correct" responses, routines and patterns of behavior. While society and its sub-groups cannot function without the traditions and rules that guide personal, social and institutional conduct, "guide" is often enacted as "restrict" or "inhibit" (Davis 1999), such that we conform and comply because of fear of flouting social norms, fear of being different, and fear of social disapproval (Khandwalla 2004). The ensuing reification which numbs our sense of agency ensures the perpetuation of these cultural blocks and limits the emergence of creativity. Indeed, cultural blocks are manifest when we fail to utilize fantasy, play, daydreaming and humor because in our culture they are not associated with serious work and hence are seen as a waste of time (Davis 1999).

Khandwalla (2004) suggests that active questioning of convention and habit, exposure to dynamic cultures, and rewarding of creative endeavors can break the confining effects of cultural blocks and of conformity and compliance. Further, a study of and interaction with people who have successfully challenged social norms is also useful.

Cognitive blocks

Mindsets/schema are cognitive frameworks that allow us to organize and process large amounts of information in an efficient manner. They serve as mental short-cuts that help us reduce the effort we put in to understand the world around us and to preserve cognitive capacity. Yet notwithstanding their utility, mindsets/schema simultaneously promote rigidity and distortions since information processing/thinking/problem solving are performed within their limits and boundaries (Baron and Byrne 2004). As a result, they hinder the cognitive transformation that creativity calls for, and much of creativity training is directed towards overcoming the blocks that emerge from mindsets/schema (Davis 1999).

Emotional blocks

Putting forth new ideas involves risk-taking and experimentation, coupled with a sense of uncertainty surrounding the outcome. While the new idea may be received with ridicule and rejection, it is also possible that the attempt to operationalize the idea may highlight the lack of feasibility and the need for reworking and refinement. Creativity thus entails facing criticism and failure as well as being able to handle complexity. The inability to cope with failure, rejection, ridicule and ambiguity, because of their association with punishment, loss, humiliation, discomfort, and uncertainty, precipitates insecurity and anxiety that impede creativity (Davis 1999; Khandwalla 2004).

The acceptance of failure as a means of growth and improvement, an accurate assessment of one's strengths and weaknesses as a basis for a resilient self-concept as well as an appreciation of the beneficial outcomes of ambiguity and complexity as opposed to the stifling effect of excessive structure and simplification are suggested avenues for overcoming this block (Khandwalla 2004).

Resource blocks

While the most common resource blocks to creativity include shortages of material and financial resources and time (Davis 1999), Khandwalla's (2004) resource myopia is an important factor. According to Khandwalla (2004), the resources at our disposal (including intrapersonal/intrapsychic resources) are much larger than we imagine and our inability to see them constitutes a common block to creativity. Resource myopia can give rise to fatalism, excessive dependence, learned helplessness and an inferiority complex, which further hamper creativity. The ability to perceive one's strengths and weaknesses accurately and the awareness of the resources in one's environment are indispensable for overcoming resource myopia (Khandwalla 2004).

THE CONFLUENCE PERSPECTIVE

Though creativity is essentially a cognitive activity, the role of facilitating and inhibitory factors in influencing its development and manifestation cannot be denied. Creative accomplishment represents the product of the combined interaction of numerous variables such as personality, environment, motivation, effort, knowledge, and so on (Feldman 1999). The contemporary confluence approach to creativity captures this multi-dimensional, holistic view. We now look at three influential models within the confluence perspective.

Amabile's componential model

Amabile's (1983, 1996a, 1996b) componential model, one of the earliest confluence approaches, proposes that creativity is the coming together of three important components, namely expertise/domain relevant skills, creativity relevant skills, and task motivation. Expertise/domain relevant skills include knowledge about, technical skills related to, and talent demanded by, the domain. Creativity relevant skills which go beyond a specific domain, being applicable to any domain in which the individual attempts to produce innovation, encompass a cognitive style favorable to taking new perspectives on problems rather than being bound by mental sets, an application of ideational techniques for the generation and exploration of alternatives, and a working style conducive to the persistent and energetic pursuit of one's work. Creativity relevant skills depend, to some extent, on personality characteristics related to independence, self-discipline, orientation towards risk-taking, tolerance for ambiguity, perseverance in the face of frustration, and a relative unconcern for social approval. Amabile (1983, 1996a, 1996b) maintains that although these two components determine what an individual is capable of doing in a given domain, it is the third component of task motivation that determines what the individual will actually do. The person's attitude towards the task and perception of his/her motivation for undertaking it are critical determinants of whether he/she will respond creatively to it. If the person finds the task intrinsically motivating (that is, if he/she is interested in the task for its own sake and is driven by deep interest and involvement in the work, curiosity, enjoyment, or a personal sense of challenge, and not because of an extrinsic/external goal/reward that is attached to its successful completion), the chances that he/she will produce a creative response are maximized. Extrinsic motivation has a negative effect on creativity. Further, if the person believes that he/she has independently chosen to work on the task, the outcome will be more creative than if he/she is working on the task because of external pressures.

Amabile (1983, 1996a, 1996b) asserts that the three components of expertise/domain relevant skills, creativity relevant skills and task motivation are necessary and sufficient conditions for creative work. An individual's level on these components determines his/her creative performance on a task, and the absence of even one component implies that creativity is not possible.

Sternberg and Lubart's investment model

According to Sternberg and Lubart (1991), the confluence of six distinct but interrelated resources possessed by an individual (also known as an individual's portfolio) has the potential to result in creativity, if the individual invests them appropriately in a task.

These resources include (*i*) specific aspects of intelligence including the synthetic ability to define and represent problems in new ways, the analytic ability to recognize which ideas are worth pursuing, and the practical ability to persuade others of the value of one's new ideas; (*ii*) knowledge of a field such that one is not closed or entrenched but sufficiently well-versed with the field to be able to move it forward; (*iii*) thinking styles which encompass a preference for thinking in novel ways of one's own choosing and a preference for working with the big picture rather than with the details; (*iv*) personality attributes including, but not limited to, self-efficacy, perseverance, openness to new experiences, individuality, willingness to take sensible risks, ability to challenge conventions, and ability to tolerate ambiguity; (*v*) motivation which could be either intrinsic or extrinsic but energizes the person and allows him/her to focus on the task; and (*vi*) an environment that provides physical and social stimulation to generate and nurture ideas.

The creative person employs the resources in his/her portfolio to first "buy low", that is, to pursue ideas that are new or out of favor but have potential. After developing these ideas, the person moves on to "sell high", that is, to present the outcome of his/her endeavor publicly, at the right moment and in the right way, so that it may be appreciated and accepted. Having successfully completed the cycle, the creative person reinitiates the process, turning his/her attention to the next round of "buying low" (Sternberg and Lubart 1991).

Sternberg and Lubart (1999) specify that creativity involves more than just a simple sum of a person's attained level of functioning for each resource. Not only are there thresholds for some resources (for example knowledge) below which creativity is not possible regardless of the levels attained on other resources, but also partial compensation may occur in which a strength on one resource (for example motivation) counteracts a weakness on another resource (for example environment). Moreover, interactions may also occur between resources, such as intelligence and motivation, in which high levels on both could multiplicatively enhance creativity.

Csikszentmihalyi's systems model

In the light of historical evidence that indicated that flashes of insight were but one step in a creative process that often took years and that judgments of creativity were related to social attributions within specific contexts, Csikszentmihalyi (1988) proposed that creativity resided in a systemic process, where three subsystems comprising domain, field and individual, linked through circular causality, equifinality and synergy, jointly give rise to creativity. That is, the field selects from the novel changes/variations produced by individuals, those variations that it deems worthy of preserving; the domain incorporates the selections of the field and transmits them to future generations; and the individual, who after gaining familiarity with the domain, brings about some novel change in it.

Given the critical contribution of each subsystem to the process of creativity, it is impossible to study these parts in isolation: without a domain, an individual would have nowhere to start from; and without a field to evaluate an individual's ideas, there would be no way to differentiate what is creative from what is banal or bizarre. Each subsystem, thus, provides an important component in the process of creativity. The domain provides the set of rules and procedures that comprise a specific symbolic context and is nested in the shared knowledge of a culture. When an individual introduces a novel variation into a domain, members of a field act as gatekeepers of the domain, deciding if the new idea is worthy to be selected and preserved. While domains and fields are essential to the process of creativity, the creative person is equally indispensable. It is the person's novel idea that gives members of a field the opportunity to include it in the domain. Such a person should have aesthetic sensibilities that help in finding problems, broad interests and openness to new ideas, the drive to bring order and meaning to experience, unique life experiences and reflective insight, disciplined work habits, the ability to have deep emotional experiences and get absorbed in tasks, relatively high intelligence, and flexible cognitive styles that negotiate tensions between various needs, such as the need for social contact and the need for solitary reflection (Csikszentmihalyi 1988; Csikszentmihalyi and Rathunde 1998).

The strength of confluence models lies in their capacity to cohesively integrate diverse findings about the nature of creativity. Moreover, these models can account for intra-individual and inter-individual differences in creativity. Yet, because confluence models include numerous dimensions and interactions between these dimensions, they lack parsimony and specificity, besides being difficult to test (Lubart 1999).

Part II

Getting Oriented

Having understood the basic concepts associated with creativity as detailed in Part I of this book, the stage is now set to move into the training component included in Part II. The training component comprises five modules to be executed as workshops, each of which should be held on a single day over five consecutive weeks. Each workshop lasts for about six hours and is followed up with take-home assignments that provide participants with practice in creative thinking.

Initiating the process of ideation, Module 1 provides participants with a basic understanding of creativity, drawing on Part I of the book. Modules 2 to 5 cover specific creativity techniques, and introductory notes included here provide instructors with background material to familiarize themselves with each technique. The role of facilitators and inhibitors has been woven in too. Facilitators and inhibitors are directly addressed through workshop activities and take-home assignments encompassing self-exploration, self-awareness, self-efficacy, changing mindsets and heightened ecological sensitivity. While the instructor must provide an environment of support and constructive feedback that not only reinforces the fact that everyone is creative but also encourages risk-taking, eliminates ridicule and appropriately suspends judgment, the targeting of a management/business audience presumes adequate knowledge of the domain.

Activities and resources for each workshop are provided in complete detail and in sequence, such that a step-by-step training program may be conducted. The introductory note included in each module may be given to the participants at the end of the workshop as a reading handout. Problems and cases from other sources may be used as substitutes instead of those provided in this book.

Additional resources that the instructor will have to arrange for include:

(1) Classrooms with whiteboards/blackboards and markers/chalks.
(2) Computers with Microsoft Office and projector facilities.

(3) Compact Discs (CDs) and CD players.

(4) Art material and stationery items, as required for the particular activity.

(5) Picture and word force fitting trigger cards, developed on the lines indicated in Module 3.

(6) Photocopies of worksheets, reflections sheets, reading handouts and take-home assignments.

During the workshops, background music may be played, should this be collectively agreed upon by the group.

It is best to work with a group of 24 to 30 people—at all times, the size of the class should be in even numbers since activities and exercises are planned on these lines. For group activities, separate classrooms with blackboards/whiteboards, music playing facilities, computer facilities, and specific resources required for the activity should be arranged for each group.

Performance of participants during workshops and in take-home assignments is to be evaluated essentially on the lines of Guilford's (1950) four principles of divergent thinking, namely, flexibility, fluency, originality and elaboration. Principles of specific techniques may be engaged, as required.

While fluency represents the number of ideas generated, flexibility examines the range of themes/categories the ideas fall into, and elaboration looks at the completeness of the ideas. Originality is assessed by determining the degree of uniqueness of the idea (Runco 1999b).

For take-home assignments 1–4, a duration of one week may be allotted to complete the exercises. Take-home assignment 5 may be allotted two weeks.

While participants are expected to maintain personal reflections, using the reflections sheets provided during each workshop as aids in this process, they may be asked to submit a personal reflections note at the end of the course (approximately one week after the completion of Workshop 5), highlighting their learnings and experiences.

A creativogenic environment should be maintained throughout the course so that participants experience a safe space where they can break the rules without sanctions as well as gain a positive perspective on

themselves and a supportive response to their efforts. Offering participants a context in which they can test the limits of the acceptable, without risk or feelings of guilt, ridicule and failure, would foster in them the
courage to deviate from what everyone else is doing (Cropley 1999).

The issues focused on in the exercises primarily emphasize
organizations/management/business. Activities relating to the self
are included in order to address both facilitators and inhibitors. The
adoption of general items to provide practice with ideation has been
deliberately done to incorporate diversity and mental flexibility in the
learning process, based on the premise that random stimulation triggers cross-fertilization, and in turn, better ideation. Cases are included
in this book for the purpose of applying and learning the use of creative thinking techniques and not to illustrate effective or ineffective
handling of a situation. Except for the case of Cochin Port, names of
organizations and of people associated with the other cases included
in this book have been changed to maintain confidentiality.

Module 1

Initiating Ideation

INTRODUCTORY NOTE: WHAT IS CREATIVITY?

Creativity is a cognitive activity that engages a range of mental abilities and processes, such as remembering, imagining, planning, anticipating, judging, organizing, storing, deciding, determining, perceiving, comprehending, learning, recognizing and interpreting (Martinsen and Kaufmann 1999; Weisberg 2006), but its essential distinguishing features are problem redefinition and ideation. Redefining the problem provides the opportunity to look at a problem from different viewpoints, allowing diverse perspectives not immediately available to us, to come to the fore. Ideation involves the generation of alternatives, triggered via the use of the imagination, associational thinking and other generative processes such as conceptual combination, analogical transfer, and so on. Problem redefinition and ideation allow novel and unique ideas to emerge. They are followed by evaluation which ensures the usefulness of the ideas.

The mental processes described above result in creative outcomes. While creative outcomes could be manifest as products, processes or thoughts, they are necessarily characterized by three dimensions: originality/uniqueness/novelty, appropriateness/relevance/effectiveness/utility and ethics. Genuine creativity goes beyond mere novelty to respond appropriately to the issue at hand without causing harm (Cropley 1999; Khandwalla 2004). Outrageous ideas and non-conforming acts (Cropley 1999) as well as contrarian inclinations (Runco 1999a) that neither address the issue at stake nor serve the interests of society, are not defined as creative (Amabile and Tighe 1993; Cropley 1999; Runco 1999a). Creative outcomes must thus contribute a relevant and effective novelty that benefits society. As MacKinnon (1970) has indicated, the novelty of a product is not enough to justify its being called creative. Instead, the novel product must solve a problem and fit the needs of a given situation.

Creativity, then, is a complex phenomenon, encompassing both process and outcome. Drawing from and elaborating on the cognitive perspective outlined above, I define creativity as a cognitive activity falling in the realms of thinking, problem solving and information processing, that engages problem redefinition and ideation processes, followed by an evaluative component, to give rise to outcomes which are original, useful and ethical. As Khandwalla (2004) maintains, creativity is neither just the production of something novel and useful, because this could have occurred as a result of convergent cognitive activities, nor is it a mere mental process that sees linkages between unrelated ideas emerging from imagination and ideation, because if that was the case then dreaming would constitute creativity. On the contrary, creativity is the employment of a playfully exploratory rather than a mechanical process of problem solving, to find solutions that are novel and yet appropriate to the context (Khandwalla 2004).

Creativity is alternatively termed as innovation and these nomenclatures are synonymous and interchangeable (see for example Harvard Business School 2003; Van de Ven 1986; West and Rickards 1999), though some scholars distinguish innovation as being the successful implementation of creative ideas (Amabile 1996a; Khandwalla 2003; West and Rickards 1999).

LEVELS OF CREATIVITY

Guilford's (1950) view that creativity is a universal phenomenon has been endorsed by numerous experts who recognize that everyone can be creative, though not necessarily in the same way or to the same degree (Nickerson 1999). Evidence that all of us are capable of being creative becomes apparent when we are faced with new problems for which we have no ready solution and have to come up with one on our own.

Numerous typologies have been put forward to demonstrate the view that creativity is distributed across the population in varying degrees. Cropley (1999), for instance, distinguishes between the ordinary creativity of everyday life in which most people produce ideas or products that are new for them at their level; and sublime creativity or the production of great works that are novel in the sense that they are widely hailed as enlarging human perspectives in some way not previously seen in history.

Ripple (1999) discusses two classifications, namely, the capital "C" versus small "c" typology and the psychological "P" versus historical "H" levels of creativity. Capital "C" creativity is a genius view which sees creativity as the special province of special individuals at rare moments in historical time. It involves bringing into existence something genuinely new that receives social validation and is valued enough to be added to culture. In contrast, small "c" creativity is specific to the individual, entailing ideas or products which are new to just that person. "P" creativity is conceptualized on the same lines as small "c" creativity, referring to ideas that are new to that person, irrespective of how many other people may have had that idea. H creativity refers to ideas that are new for the whole of human history (Ripple 1999).

CREATIVITY AS A COGNITIVE ACTIVITY

The essential distinguishing features of creativity as a cognitive activity emerge from two processes, namely, problem redefinition and ideation (see Figure II.1). Though problem redefinition ideally precedes ideation, quite often, people attempt to ideate without redefining. Sometimes, the relationship between the two could be characterized by iteration where one starts with redefining and then moves on to ideation. If the emergent ideas do not lead towards a solution, one may return to redefining and follow it up with ideation.

Redefining the problem provides the opportunity to look at the situation from different viewpoints, allowing diverse perspectives not immediately available to us, to come to the fore. Generally, the initial way in which one looks at a problem is biased by past experience, learning, knowledge and habit, and redefinition permits alternative points of view to emerge, often leading to a holistic understanding. Redefinition takes place by looking at a problem from one perspective and then moving on to another perspective and then to still another.

Figure II.1 Creativity as a Cognitive Activity

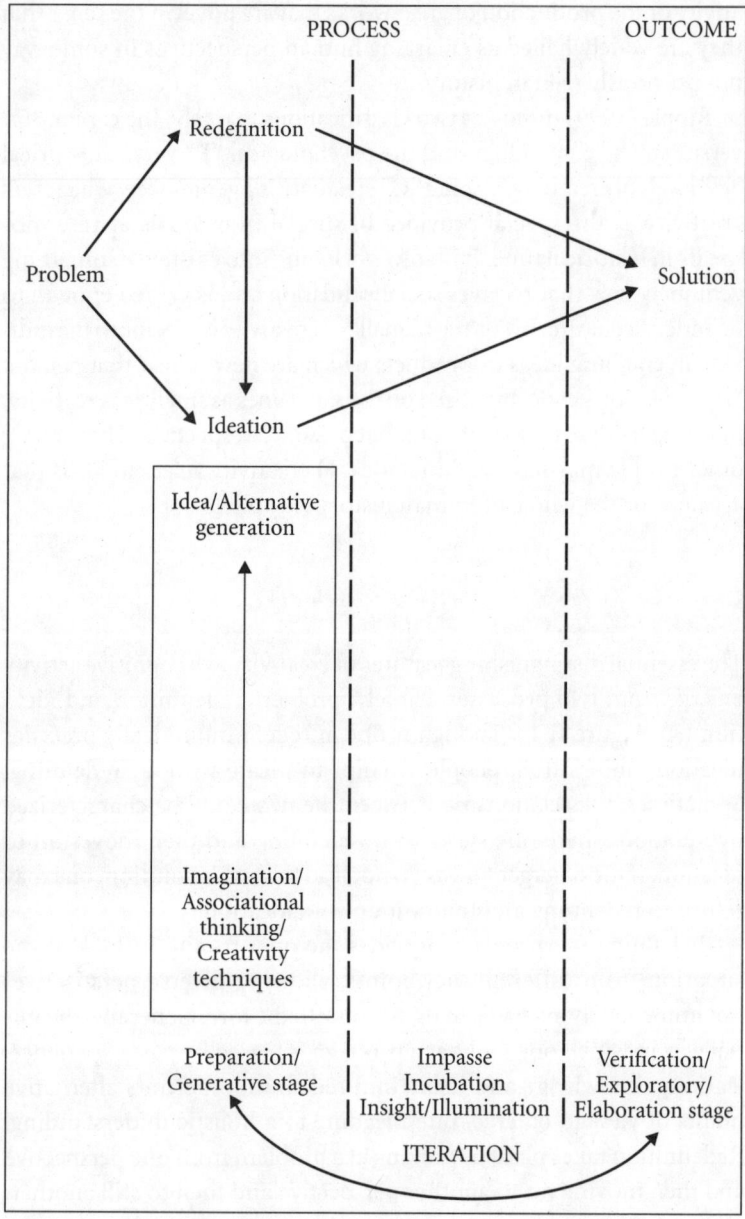

With each move, understanding deepens and one begins to comprehend the essence of the problem. In this way, one not only breaks out of the confines of existing thought processes that are limiting but also grasps the multiple and complex dimensions of the problem (Proctor 1999). This exercise, by itself, may help us solve the problem. If it does not do that, the process of redefinition any way gives direction to the process of solution generation by providing newer/different approaches to the problem.

Ideation involves the generation of alternatives, triggered via the use of the imagination (Singer 1999) and/or of associational thinking (Koestler 1964; Mednick 1962; Rothenberg 1999a, 1999b; Ward et al. 1999) and/or other generative processes (Ward et al. 1999). All of us are born with the ability to ideate but this often gets stifled during the process of socialization. Recharging, developing and maintaining the ability to ideate is possible through training in and practice with creativity techniques. Undoubtedly, ideas could vary in their novelty/uniqueness on a continuum from slightly original to highly original.

Imagination is a special feature or form of human thought characterized by the ability of the individual to reproduce images or concepts originally derived from the basic senses but now reflected in one's consciousness as memories, fantasies, or future plans. These sensory derived images can be reshaped and recombined into new images or possible future dialogues that may range from regretful ruminations about the past to rehearsals or practical planning for future anticipated events, and in some cases, to the production of creative works of art, literature or science (Singer 1999). When ideating for creativity, the imagination is encouraged to freewheel or run wild without censorship or judgment so that whatever ideas come up are retained. These ideas could be used as stimuli to develop solutions or to generate more ideas for solutions in an associational thinking process.

Associational thinking, rooted in the proposition that the mind consists entirely of ideas (words, images, formulas, and so on), each of which is associated with other ideas (Dacey 1999), is the process of linking ideas (Cropley 1999). It involves moving from one idea to another by way of a chain of associations (Dacey 1999). Suggestions for associational thinking have been put forward by numerous experts.

Mednick (1962), for example, has put forward the theory of associative hierarchies. According to him, in the course of their experiences, people learn a number of responses to a particular stimulus. These stimulus-response associations (or pairings) are developed into a hierarchy, depending on the frequency of their occurrence. Associations that occur frequently stand higher in the hierarchy with a higher probability of being selected when the stimulus recurs as compared to associations that occur infrequently. The less-likely associations are "remote" and people who make them produce unusual and unexpected ideas (Cropley 1999). Individuals with steep gradients in their hierarchy of associations tend to give more common associations and few uncommon associations while those with flat gradients give more uncommon associations and few common associations (Fasko 1999). Mednick (1962) underscored that creative individuals exhibited flat gradients in their associative hierarchies in contrast to less creative individuals whose gradients were steep. He further suggested that individuals who develop large numbers of associations for a problem have a higher probability of coming up with a creative solution. Thus, people with restricted hierarchies, in which there are one or two dominant responses, do not tend to think creatively. This is so because these responses, which occur often and quickly, block the production of less-frequent responses, resulting in stereotyped and familiar responses being made to a situation. Such people end up being at a disadvantage when novel responses (that is, relatively infrequent responses) are demanded. Creative individuals, in contrast, possess expanded associative hierarchies in which a relatively large number of responses, of more or less equal probability, are available. There is a much greater likelihood of such individuals coming up with a relatively unusual response to a situation, which could result in a creative outcome (Weisberg 2006). Mednick (1962: 221), thus, defines the creative thinking process as 'the forming of associative elements into new combinations which either meet specified requirements or are in some way useful. The more mutually remote the elements of the new combination, the more creative the process or solution'.

Koestler (1964) developed the concept of bisociation which involves combining two completely unrelated entities in such a manner that the linkage sparks off unusual ideas that result in creative breakthroughs. He contrasts this with association where related entities are linked and the ideas so emerging remain within the realm of the known and the usual. In bisociation, ideas occur in matrices or fields. Normally, ideas from the same field are combined in a process of association. However, some people combine ideas from separate matrices in a process of bisociation, which by virtue of the fact that the ideas are not normally found together, means that the combination is surprising (Cropley 1999). Koestler (1964) believes that for connections to be established via bisociation, unconscious processing is critical because this facilitates insights that break away from the confines of logic and habit. Association, on the other hand, being rooted in logic and habit, operates via conscious cognitive processes and hence does not lead to breakthroughs in thinking. Koestler (1964) cites the example of Guttenberg's invention of the printing press with movable type. Guttenberg's idea resulted from his visit to a wine festival where he realized that the press used to crush grapes could be used to apply type to paper. Thus, the movable-type printing press was born.

Rothenberg (1999a, 1999b) suggests homospatial and janusian processes as means of developing associations. The homospatial process consists of actively conceiving two or more discrete identities occupying the same space, a conception leading to the articulation of new identities. In this process, concrete entities such as rivers, houses, rockets, animals, human faces, and so on as well as sensory data such as sound patterns, visual images, tactile sensations and written words are brought together in the mind such that they totally fill its perceptual space, stimulating, as a result, unusual ideas (Rothenberg 1999a). He elaborates via an example. A poet produced the metaphor "the branches were handles of stars" through a homospatial process where the shared sound qualities and the shared shapes of the wooden objects "branch" and "handle" led him to believe that they ought to be together and hence he superimposed them in his mind. As the poet experienced a vivid impression of the letter "a" overlapping in the two words, the idea of stars was generated, and the metaphor was created (Rothenberg 1999a).

The janusian process, derived from the qualities of the Roman god, Janus, who had faces that looked in multiple diametrically opposite directions simultaneously, consists of actively yet concomitantly conceiving multiple opposites or antitheses. During the course of the creative process, opposite or antithetical ideas, concepts, or propositions are consciously conceptualized as simultaneously coexisting. Although seemingly illogical and self-contradictory, these formulations are constructed in clearly logical and rational states of mind to produce creative effects. They occur as early conceptions in the development of scientific theories and artworks and at critical junctures at middle and later stages as well. Because they serve generative functions during both formative and critical stages of the creative process, these simultaneous antitheses or opposites usually undergo transformation and modification and are seldom directly discernible in final created products. They are formulated by the creative thinker as solutions in working out practical and scientific tasks and as central ideas for artwork (Rothenberg 1999b).

Other generative processes include the retrieval of existing structures from memory, the formation of simple associations among those structures or combinations of them, the mental synthesis of new structures, the mental transformation of existing structures into new forms, conceptual combination and expansion/extension, analogical transfer of information from one domain to another, and categorical reduction in which existing structures are conceptually reduced to more primitive constituents (Ward et al. 1999).

Both problem redefinition and ideation abilities can be developed, enhanced and internalized through training and practice with creativity techniques such as brainstorming, morphological analysis, lateral thinking and synectics, and their variants.

Problem redefinition and ideation are aligned with divergent thinking, that is, the ability to find substantial numbers of new, original and unexpected answers, generally to loosely defined problems for which there is no prior correct solution (Guilford 1950), and this is characterized as imaginative, uninhibited, inventive, unpredictable, and revolutionary (Nickerson 1999), with the quality of the output being judged from the perspectives of Guilford's (1950) principles of fluency, flexibility and originality.

Fluency refers to the number of ideas that a person is able to come up with in order to solve a given problem. The more ideas a person can generate, the more ideationally fluent he/she is. For example, if a group of people are asked to list the number of uses a coaster can serve, those listing a higher number will be considered to be more ideationally fluent that those listing a smaller number.

Flexibility takes into account the range of themes or categories encompassed by the ideas generated. The greater the range of themes or categories covered, the higher the flexibility demonstrated. In the instance of coasters referred to above, the person providing five uses of coasters as a dining/beverage device exemplifies the absence of flexibility in contrast to the flexibility shown by the person whose five uses of coasters include a wall-hanging, a bookmark, a fashion accessory, a tool for sports and games, and a lampshade.

Originality emphasizes the ability to come up with unusual, unique, novel, and innovative ideas as potential solutions to a given problem. In the case of coasters, their use as earrings or knee pads may be considered unusual, and therefore, original responses. A related ability is the ability to come up with novel relationships between ideas.

For problem redefinition and ideation to be effective, suspension of judgment/evaluation is mandatory. This is so because it is only by withholding judgment/evaluation that a free and uninhibited generation and flow of wild and remote ideas is facilitated. As a result, a greater number of and more unusual and unique ideas emerge and are retained. This not only increases the pool from which potential solutions can be drawn but also serves as stimulation for breeding further ideas.

The processes of problem redefinition and ideation described above correspond with the generative phase of Finke et al.'s (1992) geneplore model and with the preparation phase of Wallas's (1926) stage model (see Figure II.1).

As mentioned earlier, problem redefinition and/or ideation provide potential solutions for the problem situation. The initial ideas generated during this time are sometimes described as pre-inventive in the sense that they are not complete but rather may be an untested proposal or even a mere germ of an idea, but they hold some promise of responding to the situation at hand (Ward et al. 1999). In other words, initial ideas could be wild/remote and impractical/unfeasible. They need to be followed up with the exploratory (Finke et al. 1992) or verification (Wallas 1926) stage, characterized essentially by convergent thinking in which alternatives are evaluated and appropriately developed to meet the demands of the problem situation (see Figure II.1).

Convergent thinking which includes categorization, logical thinking, analysis, comparison, evaluation, and so on (Khandwalla 2004), is associated with well-defined, structured problems which have prior correct solutions (Ripple 1999). Convergent thinking emphasizes logic, reality, practicality, conservatism and dependability (Nickerson 1999) and can be regarded as the mental abilities that facilitate the assessment and elaboration of an innovative solution (Khandwalla 2004).

Guilford (1950) considers elaboration to be the key principle during the exploratory/verification stage. According to him, elaboration, which is indispensable in putting a creative idea to work, comprises the ability to add detail and depth to complete an idea and has also been recognized as a significant creative ability. Csikszentmihalyi and Sawyer (1995) provide evidence for the verification/exploratory stage. They state that after an idea is reached, it needs to be shaped and evaluated to fit reality, a process they term elaboration.

The transition from the generative/preparation stage to the exploratory/verification/elaboration stage need not proceed smoothly. In other words, it is possible that the ideas generated via problem redefinition and ideation do not lend themselves to appropriate and useful solutions and hence a return to the generative/preparatory stage becomes inevitable. In this manner, iteration between the preparation/ generative and exploratory/verification/elaboration stages continues until a solution is finalized (see Figure II.1).

It is important to recognize that even the iterative process between the preparation/generative and the exploratory/verification/elaboration stages may not be immediately successful in finding a solution to the problem. Instead, it may face an impasse during which awareness of and movement towards a potential solution are blocked despite extensive problem redefinition and ideation. The resolution of an impasse involves a time lapse since it occurs after an incubation period during which the problem is temporarily put aside. Illumination/insight, which is the sudden realization of a solution that occurs either during time away from the problem, or when one returns to the problem after the incubation period, breaks the impasse and ends the incubation period (Smith and Dodds 1999). Once the impasse is resolved, and potential solutions are identified, Wallas's (1926) verification or Finke et al.'s (1992) exploratory stage follows (see Figure II.1).

That creativity calls for both divergent and convergent thinking underscores that these two processes are complementary, not antagonistic. While it was earlier believed that divergent and convergent thinking were polar opposites such that an engagement with one implied a move away from the other, the contemporary view asserts that both divergent and convergent dimensions color an individual's thinking and are equally important for problem solving (Nickerson 1999). Divergent thinking is useful for generating ideas while convergent thinking is useful for developing them further. In other words, while divergent thinking enhances the effectiveness of convergent thinking by offering more ideas to select from, convergent thinking accentuates the value of divergent thinking by making good use of the ideas generated (De Bono 1990). Undoubtedly, divergent and convergent abilities are both required in order to think effectively. To summarize in Nickerson's (1999) words, divergent thinking, at its best, generates original ideas, unusual approaches to problems and novel perspectives in terms of which to view situations while convergent thinking evaluates what divergent thinking offers, subjects the possibilities to the criteria of acceptability, and selects some from among them for further consideration.

As Figure II.1 highlights, creativity encompasses both process and outcome dimensions. That is, not only is the outcome/solution unique and novel but the process by which one arrived at it includes problem redefinition and ideation, engaging divergent thinking abilities.

It may be relevant to highlight that creativity lends itself to the resolution of all kinds of problems. While problems vary in terms of their definition, the availability of means to solve them and the clarity of the criteria for recognizing solutions, creativity is traditionally associated with non-routine or ill-defined problems which require, in the first instance, becoming aware that there is a problem at all and finding a way of defining it; second, working out techniques for solving the problem; and third, development of criteria for recognizing a solution. Such "complex" or "intractable" problems do not lend themselves to a habitual mode of problem solving, but instead, demand a high level of creativity (Cropley 1999; Mayer 1999). In contrast, clearly defined/routine problems which are solvable by means of standard techniques and which have obvious and well-known criteria for identifying solutions (Cropley 1999; Mayer 1999), are generally solved without the help of creativity, that is, we solve them in a habitual manner, relying on cognitive mechanisms and processes that we have used in the past (Mayer 1999). Yet it is important to recognize that even in these instances, though we are successful in solving the problem, it may be beneficial to explore alternatives which may provide better and more effective solutions. Creativity can thus be brought into play here too. Clearly, the opportunity to be creative is perennial, presenting itself in every facet of an individual's life through both familiar and unfamiliar experiences.

ACTIVITY SEQUENCE

(1) Christening Each Other
(2) Case Analysis
(3) Self as Creator
(4) Object Uses
(5) Word Creation
(6) Experiencing Freewheeling

CHRISTENING EACH OTHER

Instructor guidelines

Objectives

To set the tone for the course by helping participants get to know each other while simultaneously attempting to ideate. An environment relevant to and conducive for the course is also built up as a result.

Time

Thirty minutes.

Material

(1) Small strips of blank colored paper (the number should be equal to the number of participants).
(2) A large plastic/cardboard container.
(3) Blackboard with chalk/whiteboard with markers.

Procedure

(1) Distribute colored strips of paper among the participants such that each one gets one strip.

(2) Instruct the participants to write their names on the paper and then fold it and place it in the plastic bowl/cardboard box kept on the instructor's table.

(3) Ask each participant to pick up a slip of paper from the bowl/box. Looking at the name written on the paper, participants must use the alphabets of the name to create a new name in two minutes time.

(4) Once this task is completed, participants may share the names that they have created. During the sharing, participants will call out the original name on the slip of paper—this person will introduce himself/herself and then request to be told his/her new name. Once the new name has been revealed, the participant creating the new name may share how he/she came up with this name. Sharing may follow a round-robin style.

Light instrumental music may be played in the background during the activity.

CASE ANALYSIS

Instructor guidelines

Objectives

This activity is designed to make participants engage their convergent thinking skills and to later contrast the cognitive processes used here with those relied upon in creative thinking.

Time

One hour forty minutes.

Material

(1) Case analysis worksheet (the number should be equal to the number of participants).

(2) Case analysis reflections sheet (the number should be equal to the number of participants).
(3) Access to library and internet.
(4) Blackboard and chalk/whiteboard and markers.

Procedure

(1) Students may work on the case analysis, completing it in 60 minutes as per instructions.
(2) Upon completion, some students may be called to present their work or a discussion of the same may be held with the whole class. This could go on for 30 minutes.
(3) Reflections for the case analysis may then be completed by the participants in 10 minutes. Participants must retain the completed reflections sheet.

CASE ANALYSIS

Worksheet

Read the following case and answer the question at the end of it. Remember to complete the exercise in exactly the same way in which you have always solved cases. You may work individually or in a group, or you may rely essentially on yourself while engaging with group members periodically. You may use resources from the library or the internet to assist you in finding a solution.

You can take upto 60 minutes to complete this task.

Cochin Port

(This case has been developed by Professor Ernesto Noronha, Indian Institute of Management, Ahmedabad)

Cochin Port, in India's southern state of Kerala, located specifically on Willingdon Island, is an important shipping destination on India's western coast. Kochi (or Cochin)[1] was perceived to be an ideal location on the west coast to set up a transshipment hub as it is very close

---

[1] Kochi is an alternate name for Cochin.

to Colombo and it is also near the international shipping line. Yet the paucity of space on Willingdon Island hampered the development of terminals and other associated activities and hence plans were developed to expand Cochin Port. In 1984, an area of about 440 acres of land at the Vallarpadam Island was reclaimed as part of the integrated development project of Cochin Port. In 1991, the Cochin Port Trust (CoPT) prepared the first feasibility report for developing a greenfield port at Vallarpadam—this was later updated in 1998. The expectations were that once Vallarpadam was established, Cochin would be in a position to attract 80 per cent of the cargo which is transshipped from India through Colombo or Singapore.

Initial days

Since 1998, there have been several attempts made by the CoPT to get the project off the ground. In its first attempt in 1999, CoPT proposed to develop the project as a joint venture between a private operator holding 74 per cent stake and the CoPT holding the other 26 per cent. The idea was to develop the International Container Transshipment Terminal (ICTT) as a public-private partnership, where the private operator would, in the first phase, modernize the existing Rajiv Gandhi Container Terminal (RGCT) at the Cochin Port, and in the second phase, develop the ICTT, maintain it for a concession period of 30 years, and then transfer it to the government. However, this proposal faced difficulties from the very start. The intelligence bureaucracy forced CoPT to scrap the bid by Hutchison Port Holdings, citing that the Hong Kong-based group's contacts with mainland China were too close for comfort. Further, the lone price bid submitted by P&O Ports for developing the project was cancelled as this group was also involved in developing Colombo Port. It was opined that only the presence of a different operator at the Cochin Port would ensure the development of the project to its full potential as a hub port on the west coast.

Public pressure

This failure to entice enough bidders to construct the Vallarpadam project led to a lull of activity which made the people of Kerala restive. In May 2002, the Forum for Development of Kochi (a voluntary organization) organized a seminar to force the implementation of the Vallarpadam project. The forum members asserted that any delay in the implementation of the project would jeopardize the prospects of the Vallarpadam terminal as Chennai, Tuticorin and Salalah ports were adopting aggressive marketing strategies to attract customers. At the same meet, the Cochin Steamer Agents Association emphasized that Colombo Port, the major competitor to Cochin, had recently taken steps to modernize its berths so as to increase its cargo handling facility. A way out of the impasse was creating political pressure. In September 2002, trade unions in the state asserted that the state government should exert pressure on the Shipping Ministry for the early execution of the Vallarpadam Transshipment Terminal project. Similarly, in a symbolic protest, the Vishala Kochi Dweep Vikasana Samithy (Greater Cochin Island Development Committee) floated containers made of thermocol in the backwaters, protesting against the delay in implementing the proposed Vallarpadam Container Transshipment Terminal project. The committee members stated that the Indian National Rupee (INR) 20 billion project was being indefinitely delayed due to neglect on the part of India's central government. They wanted the Vallarpadam project to be implemented as it would transform the entire state of Kerala and employ thousands of unemployed youth.

Finally, in September 2002, the central government decided to re-tender the Vallarpadam Transshipment Terminal project at the Cochin Port as a full-fledged build, operate and transfer (BOT) project, using the revenue sharing format as the basis for selecting the private developer to satisfy international bidders who insisted on operational freedom. The former Union Minister for Shipping, Mr Goel, also toured Dubai, Hong Kong, Malaysia and Singapore to market the project and invite big private entities such as CSX World Terminals Limited, Hutchison Port Holdings, Dubai Ports Authority and PSA Corporation to participate in the re-tendering process.[2] P&O Ports was also allowed to bid as it was perceived that a ban on P&O Ports's participation would go against the spirit of liberalization.

On September 12, 2003, AP Moller-Maersk and CSX World Terminals Limited submitted proposals to develop the project. They stated in their proposals that the price aspect should be flexible and

---

[2] This was a National Democratic Alliance (NDA) government initiative.

open to negotiations after CoPT agrees to let the successful bidder operate the existing RGCT for at least 10 years before developing and shifting operations to the ICTT at Vallarpadam. The bidders obviously wanted to assess the market potential for the project in terms of cargo before developing the ICTT. In contrast, the CoPT had stated in its global tender for the project that the private operator should shift from the RGCT to the ICTT within five years of the award of the contract. The CoPT rejected the offers as the bidders had put several conditions while submitting the financial bids. At this stage, the CoPT suggested that the project be taken up as a national project.

Other areas of concern

In the meanwhile, other areas of concern cropped up. First, the investors had major apprehensions that the Vallarpadam area, being mainly of soft clay, would entail heavy investment for soil consolidation to withstand the heavy loads from container stacking and machineries deployed for handling containers. Second, the changes in the port and shipping industry, such as capacity addition of the existing ports, commissioning of new ports and the drastic change in ship size, required a fresh look at the traffic potential. Third, the Indian Naval authorities objected to the erection of tall Super Post Panamax cranes at the proposed Vallarpadam Transshipment Terminal project as that would come up within the flight funnel, the path of approach or take-off, posing a direct threat to aircraft flying in and out of the naval airport, especially during night flying. The Indian Navy maintained that they would give a clearance to the project only if the height of the crane was scaled down to the limits prescribed by the Airports Authority of India and the Director General of Civil Aviation. In response, the state government of Kerala announced that another hub port was to be set up at Vizhinjam just 30 kilometers south of Cochin, and the final round of bidding was expected to start at the end of July 2004. However, finally, the CoPT management, besides suggesting an alternative site at nearby Puthuvypeen, took up a soil study in the proposed site at Vallarpadam as well as a traffic update study. They also got the Defence Ministry to intervene with the Indian Navy for the final clearance of the project while the Vizhinjam project remained stillborn.

Unions' objections

Having sorted out these issues, the Cochin Port authorities began the pre-bid meeting for the third time on the proposed transshipment terminal project with potential investors. The revised tender inviting requests for proposals (RFP) for the ICTT project, incorporated the demands made by the bidders in the second round—most importantly, the demand for the transfer of RGCT to the prospective private player. This resulted in the six Cochin Port unions[3] under the banner of the Kochi Thuramukha Samrakshana Samiti (Cochin Port Protection Committee) holding demonstrations in protest against the handing over of the operations of the RGCT to private operators prior to the development of the ICTT at Cochin. The unions also sent letters to the Cochin Port trustees citing the reasons for opposing the new decision of the management to hand over RGCT to private parties. They gave notice to the port management for an indefinite strike from February 11, 2004, in protest against the neglect of the RGCT by the port management and the privatization of the terminal. At the conciliation meeting held on February 10, 2004, before the Regional Labor Commissioner (Central), the representative of the unions vehemently opposed the proposal of the management to hand over the RGCT for the establishment of the ICTT. They apprehended that this would be detrimental to the interest of the workers as well as to the port in general. They demanded that the RGCT should not be handed over to any private bidder, and should be operated by the management of CoPT. Besides this, necessary infrastructure facilities should be provided for the effective functioning of RGCT. The unions, through their publications, propagated the reason for the strike. They stated that the RGCT, which was the prime source of revenue for the port, remained in a dilapidated state. The neighboring ports bought modern

---

[3] The unions were Cochin Port Staff Association (CPSA) (close to the Congress party now leading the United Progressive Alliance (UPA) after it defeated the National Democratic Alliance (NDA) led by the Bharatiya Janata Party (BJP) in the 2004 General elections); Cochin Port Employees Organization (CPEO) (an associate of the left parties also supporting the UPA government); Cochin Thuramukha Tozhilali Union; Cochin Port and Dock Employees Union; Cochin Port Wharf Staff Association; and Cochin Port Labor Union.

equipment and handled goods efficiently while the CoPT operated with outdated equipment. In order to facilitate the privatization of the port, the central government and the CoPT were not interested in buying any equipment or maintaining the existing machinery. In spite of the capacity of the terminal being 95,000 twenty-foot equivalent units (TEUs) per year, 165,000 TEUs were handled due to the active participation of the workers and the net revenue from operations in the year 2003 was INR 250 million. The unions argued that on March 19, 2003, the Board of CoPT decided to buy new cranes and equipment and to invest in the maintenance of the terminal. However, the central government ordered the CoPT to refrain from any further expenditure since their intention was to hand over the terminal to private parties. The order note also stated that the third bid conditions were that the private operator had to handle 400,000 TEUs in four years after which, they would start work on the Vallarpadam project. If this condition was not met, they could operate the RGCT for another 24 months and withdraw from the project by paying INR 100 million as compensation to the port. All this, according to the unions, clearly indicated the bidders were exploiting the situation and were not really interested in developing the Vallarpadam project. The bidders could withdraw by paying only a nominal amount of compensation for the utilization of RGCT. The security of the workers was still undecided while the government endeavored to sell national property to private parties, the unions alleged.

After a lengthy discussion and with the persuasion of the conciliation officer, the unions agreed to defer the proposed strike of February 11, 2004, on the understanding that the RFP, then published by the CoPT in connection with the bid process of Cochin International Container Transshipment Terminal, was a draft one and not a final RFP, and that a final decision would be taken only after further processing of the issue by the authorities and subsequent approval by the Board of CoPT. It was further agreed by the management that, prior to formulating a final decision, they would discuss the proposal to hand over the RGCT to the successful bidder of the ICTT project for operations and related matters, with the trade unions who had served strike notices, and arrive at a mutually agreed settlement.

The third bid

Nonetheless, the CoPT issued notices inviting tenders for the third time. Seven international and local bidders were short-listed, subject to security clearance, for the building of the proposed hub terminal. However, only three submitted their bids. The CoPT opened the financial bids on March 25, 2004. Dubai Ports International (DPI), the global arm of the Dubai Ports Authority (DPA), emerged as the highest bidder for the ICTT project at CoPT. The DPI's quote of 33.3 per cent revenue sharing with the Cochin Port was the highest. Besides this, it would also pay INR 400 million for the equipment and an annual licence fee of INR 96 million. The other bidders like IL&FS-Punj Lloyd quoted 10.1 per cent revenue sharing while A P Moller-Maersk submitted only a few conditions, the same stand that it had adopted in the previous round of bidding. Unlike in the first bid, the private operator was allowed to start developing the new port only after managing to push up traffic at the RGCT from the existing 170,000 TEUs to 400,000 TEUs, or after eight years of takeover, whichever happened first. The prospective operator was also allowed to pay for the costs of the existing equipment in installments rather than having to make an upfront payment. In addition, the government offered assistance in the form of "viability gap funding" for creating common user infrastructure facilities such as national highway connectivity, rail connectivity, dredging and providing break-waters, at a total cost of INR 9320 million.

CoPT management made some relaxations in the tender conditions stipulated for the project. The flexibility of conditions offered by the port included an extension of the period to set up the project at the Vallarpadam site after taking over RGCT, an installment-based payment of the upfront fee, the minimum net worth of the applicant was fixed at US$ 80 million as against US$ 200 million earlier, the aggregate cash accruals of the applicant for the last three financial years was reduced to 1/4th of US$ 40 million from US$ 100 million, and the applicant was now also required to manage and operate one or more container terminals with an annual combined through-put of not less than 500,000 TEUs as compared to 1,500,000 TEUs earlier. The port also agreed to expand the container stacking yard in the port premises. Moreover, to make private participation in the proposed Vallarpadam

Transshipment Terminal project attractive, the CoPT sought the permission of the Union Commerce Ministry to convert the area into a Special Economic Zone (SEZ). The SEZ would be deemed as a foreign territory for the purpose of trade and tariffs. All imports into the SEZ would be duty-free and there would be only minimum Customs' formality. There would be no Customs' examination of import and export, and investment approvals, even for 100 per cent Foreign Direct Investment (FDI) owned projects, would be obtained from Cochin. As of now, the SEZ would be a reformulation of the container hub and would include the 150 acres of land on the Vallarpadam Island where the new terminal was proposed to be set up. The entire area would be developed into a Customs' bonded area. It would have an international transshipment terminal, bunkering facilities, ship repair facilities, shopping malls, golf courses, warehouses, and processing facilities. Apart from these, the Special Purpose Vehicle (SPV) set up for creating the SEZ would be exempted from income tax for 10 years under Section 81(A) of the Income Tax Act, making the project attractive to potential investors. Infrastructure investments within the SEZ were exempted from customs duty in case of imports and from excise duties and sales tax in case of purchases from the domestic market. This would cut investment costs by 35 per cent.

Unions relent

In the meanwhile, Cochin Port Staff Association (CPSA), one of the main unions in the port, changed its stance and supported the privatization move at the CoPT board meeting on March 4, 2004. However, the Cochin Port Employees Organization (CPEO), the other major union in the port, opposed privatization more vehemently and saw it as a betrayal. It stated that in the present bid, there was no penalty clause. In its dissent note as one of the trustees of the CoPT, CPEO raised doubts about achieving the target of 400,000 TEUs since Kerala did not generate cargo and was uncertain about the working conditions of the employees. The CPEO union leader stated that the CoPT could build the ICTT on its own, by taking a loan from the Asian Development Bank (ADB) or from other ports that had a surplus, as suggested by the government earlier. They also stated that on September 19, 2003, the CoPT board had taken a decision that funds should be raised from other parties such as the ADB or other ports instead of depending on a private agency. This was struck down by the National Democratic Alliance (NDA) government in the name of being investor friendly. The CPEO (while lamenting that the CPSA had changed its stand in support of the development of Vallarpadam), stuck to its guns and was sure that its Left Democratic Front (LDF) Members of Parliament (MPs) would not allow the privatization of Cochin port. However, soon after the general elections in May 2004, the CPEO too did an about-turn. The pressure of public opinion that some selfish trade unions were delaying the implementation of the project (which was expected to create thousands of jobs) forced it to alter its position. The CPEO now began to espouse public interest and worker sacrifice, and moved away from its rigid stand to ensure that the port did not face closure. Moreover, it claimed that it was the pressure from the Left MPs that resulted in the implementation of the project.

A divided workforce

In spite of these developments, workers were unsure as to whether privatization would actually occur and whether the takeover would actually happen. This was because one of the union leaders had told them that only after the letter of intent was sent, the action would begin; until then, privatization would remain a distant possibility.

Notwithstanding this uncertainty, workers remained divided in their views about the pros and cons of privatization. One group was steadfast in its resolve against privatization. The logic of selling public sector companies to the private sector was questioned. The argument was that "if these units were not viable why was the private sector interested in buying them?" Some of the workers hinted at corruption, going to the extent of saying that there was a deliberate attempt to convert the profit making units into loss making ones.

They suggested that instead of privatizing the port, the profits of CoPT could be ploughed back to fund the terminal construction or Mumbai Port could be induced to invest in Cochin port. If profits could be made in spite of the complete indifference of the port authorities to investment in equipment, then handing over the RGCT to the DPA was not advantageous. Indeed, ports were considered to be a vital organ of the nation.

This group of workers remained skeptical about employment conditions and opportunities. They believed that capital intensive, rather than labor intensive, technology would be used. Workers also espoused fears of redundancy as privatization would result in contract workers replacing them. They foresaw a change in the workload and manning scale due to privatization. The culture of freedom that was intrinsically linked to job security was on the verge of being lost. Older employees suggested that they were too old for the DPA to even consider them. The fear of losing their long term benefits seemed to grip them. Further, privatization would put a stop to "speed money",[4] resulting in a financial crisis. Workers' insecurity about their jobs had an impact on how DPA officials were perceived when they visited the port to inspect the equipment. Workers' self-worth dipped considerably when they were ignored by DPA officials during the latter's visits to the port. Not surprisingly, workers preferred to work for the government rather than for the private sector. However, the Chennai Port strike[5] did provide them with some strength. They believed that it was possible to strike even when working in the private sector.

The workers were not sure of being deputed or being made permanent employees of the DPA. Obviously, most of them were interested in moving over to the DPA only on deputation so that their benefits, like pension (that they were eligible for as employees of CoPT), remained intact. Moreover, they also wanted the option of choosing to be deputed. However, they were not confident about the deputation because they alleged that the union had not updated them on earlier occasions on the issue of housestuffing. The workers also tried to get themselves posted elsewhere in the port. They termed the entire operation of privatization as Darwinian, invoking the notion of survival of the fittest.

---

[4] Extra amount paid, beyond wages, for loading and unloading operations or for release of goods from warehouses in almost all Indian ports. Speed money is often considered illegal (Noronha 2005).

[5] This was the first major scuffle between Chennai Container Terminal Ltd (CCTL) management and its workers after the terminal was privatized in November 2001. Workers were demanding a raise in salary and reinstatement of four suspended colleagues. They also alleged 'ill treatment'—like threats of suspension—by the CCTL management, which, however, was disputed by the management.

The other group of workers viewed privatization more favorably. Though they expressed concerns about their job security, they recognized that privatization was the only means by which the Cochin Port would survive and compete effectively since the government did not have the funds to invest in big projects such as Vallarpadam. These workers believed that their sacrifices would ensure the prosperity of future generations. They also believed that the DPA would bring more work to the port because of its networks with other corporate organizations. Further, systematic organization of work and of the container yard as well as utilization of modern technology and equipment, both of which would reduce work-related stress, were cited as other benefits of privatization.

Clearly, there was a division among the workers.

Chairman's intervention

To allay the workers' fears, the Chairman of CoPT addressed the workers through the official organization bulletin and answered their questions in an open house organized by the Bharatiya Mazdoor Sangh (BMS).[6] The Chairman, in his communication to the workers in February 2004, tried to convey the rationale behind establishing the transshipment terminal, to assuage the fears of job insecurity and to explain the future of the RGCT. It was emphasized that if the container operations did not start immediately, the potential benefit would shift to other ports. Vallarpadam would provide employment opportunities in Kerala, and for this to be realized, the involvement and participation of workers was essential. A number of points were highlighted: Cochin Port is near the international shipping line and has the potential of being a transshipment hub. The government was unable to invest a huge sum in the project and therefore a private operator has to step in. The private operator would share revenues with the CoPT and transparency would be maintained as the operator had to match the movement of containers with the Customs' statements. The RGCT would be handed over to the operator, who would start the Vallarpadam project as soon as 400,000 TEUs were handled. The private operator could even start construction before this, and it would be a great loss for the operator

---

[6] A trade union that is closely affiliated to the Bharatiya Janata Party (BJP).

if they failed to implement the project or if they maintained business below 400,000 TEUs as the annual fee was to be paid in advance. The Chairman also clarified that when the private operator takes over the container terminal, the existing 361 employees of the container terminal would be transferred to the private operator and the wages, allowances and bonus of these employees would in no way be inferior to those earned at the time of transfer. In addition, the private operator would be liable not only for the transferred employees' pension and leave salary contribution, but these employees and their dependents would also continue to avail of the facility of the CoPT hospital at the cost of the operator. In short, the private operator could improve on the existing benefits but would not be allowed to impose poorer conditions. Moreover, when the private operator shifted to Vallarpadam, the container terminal employees would return to CoPT.

Nonetheless, a climate of suspicion, doubt, anxiety and fear continued to grip the workers.

Your task

How would you deal with the situation at Cochin Port?

CASE ANALYSIS

Reflections sheet

Take a few minutes to recollect and note down your thoughts, feelings and actions while working on the case of Cochin Port. The following questions will give you some leads but are not meant to be exhaustive.

(1) How did I proceed to solve the problem at hand?
(2) How did I go about identifying and developing solutions?
(3) Were there any factors influencing me?
(4) What were my thoughts about and what did they lead me to do?
(5) What were my feelings during various stages of the problem solving process—and how did they contribute to my task completion?

(6) What resources/supports (including intrapersonal ones) did I rely on during this exercise?

(7) Was I conscious of what I was doing/thinking/feeling during this time?

SELF AS CREATOR

Instructor guidelines

Objectives

This activity helps participants explore themselves as creative beings. It allows them to get in touch with themselves, examining instances where they have been creative in the past and exploring their desire to be creative in the future. Aspects of their self-concept that facilitate and inhibit this process are delved into.

The activity also introduces and emphasizes the fact that all human beings can be creative, though in differing degrees, and that with exposure to creativity training, this ability can be developed.

Time

Fifty minutes.

Material

(1) Self as Creator worksheet (the number should be equal to the number of participants).

(2) Course outline (the number should be equal to the number of participants).

Procedure

(1) A class room discussion may be initiated with the question "How many of you think of yourself as creative?" Based on a show of hands, the questions "Why" and "Why not" may be asked. Participants may share their experiences, if they wish to.

(2) The instructor then encourages participants to explore themselves further by filling out the "Self as creator" worksheet— 20 minutes may be set aside for this.

(3) The activity is wrapped up with a discussion of the different levels of creativity, of personality factors that facilitate creativity and of creative self-efficacy.

(4) Following this, the instructor introduces the participants to the course, its objectives, its scope and its pedagogy. The course outline may be distributed at this stage.

SELF AS CREATOR

Worksheet

Identify any/all experience(s) in your life where you have been creative.

....
....
....

Think about yourself a little bit and examine the different facets of yourself (personality/traits/abilities/interests/attitudes) that make/can make you a creative person?

....
....
....

Are there any facets of yourself which are inhibiting you from becoming a creative person? Which are these?

....
....
....

What has been the role of your environment/experiences in facilitating/ inhibiting your creativity—any significant experience/event that has caused you to be more/less creative?

....
....
....

Facilitators

....

....

....

Inhibitors

....

....

....

CREATIVE THINKING AT THE WORKPLACE: COURSE OUTLINE

Course objectives

(1) To develop an understanding of creativity as a cognitive activity.
(2) To learn and internalize creativity skills, with a view to applying them in organizational settings.

Pedagogy and scope

The course comprises five modules covering creativity techniques, facilitators and blocks, that will be conducted through workshops. Workshop exercises, personal reflections and take-home assignments are designed to help participants develop the habit of thinking creatively and look at themselves as creative individuals. As a result of these inputs, participants should acquire not just a different, but enlarged, repertoire of cognitive skills which they use more consciously, but they should also view themselves as creative individuals. The latter transformation is possible only if the participant works actively towards it by being conscious of his/her cognitions/feelings/actions not just during the workshops but even during the intervening periods in the course of all his/her waking behaviors. This consciousness sets into motion a feedback process, which in turn stimulates self-correction and behavior change, culminating in internalization and an altered self. Achieving this, of course, calls for a prolonged self-involvement which includes the conscious use of the techniques and greater self-awareness about one's general predisposition and orientation.

Course material, including readings, worksheets and other resources, will be provided by the instructor during the course of the workshops.

Modules

(1) Module 1: Initiating Ideation
(2) Module 2: Thinking Laterally
(3) Module 3: Relayering
(4) Module 4: Fantasy Trails
(5) Module 5: Essential Brainstorming

The instructor can build in a component of evaluation on the lines indicated below:

(1) Workshop participation: 30 per cent
(2) Take-home assignments: 30 per cent
(3) Personal reflections: 20 per cent
(4) Conceptual quiz: 20 per cent

OBJECT USES

Instructor guidelines

Objectives

This activity is designed to introduce participants to the principles of originality, fluency and flexibility. Through the game of passing the parcel, each participant gets an object and has to come up with as many unusual uses for the object as possible.

Time

Forty minutes.

Material

(1) A bag filled with objects of everyday life (such as paper weights, pens, combs, batteries, glasses, CDs, and so on). Please note that there should be one object per participant. Avoid duplicating an object.
(2) Music.
(3) Prize for the winner.

Procedure

(1) Make all the participants form a circle.
(2) Participants must pass the object bag sequentially when the music begins to play. The person holding the object bag when the music stops must pick out an object from the bag and must step aside. He/she should retain the object till further instructions are provided.
(3) Continue with the passing process till there are two people left. At this stage, when the music stops, the person who manages to pass on the bag is the winner and may be given a prize. Allow both these people to pick up an object from the bag.
(4) Tell all the participants to note down in five minutes as many unusual uses as they can for the object they have picked.
(5) Invite participants to share their ideas.
(6) Wrap up the activity by introducing the concept of divergent thinking, using participants' output in the current exercise as illustrations.

WORD CREATION

Instructor guidelines

Objectives

The attempt in this exercise is to build on the understanding of divergent thinking introduced in the last activity. Here, the focus is on originality, with participants being given a feel of inventing something of their own, setting the stage for the rest of the course. Apart from sowing the seeds of creative self-efficacy in participants, this activity initiates the process of ideation.

Time

Thirty minutes.

Material

(1) Small strips of blank colored paper (the number should be equal to the number of participants).
(2) A large plastic/cardboard container.
(3) Blackboard with chalk/whiteboard with markers.

Procedure

(1) Distribute the small strips of colored paper among the participants.
(2) Ask them to invent a new science "…ology" including a name and a definition in five minutes.
(3) They may write the name on the colored paper and place it in the container on the instructor's table.
(4) Once everyone has completed this, the instructor may call out the newly created words one by one and ask the inventor to define the word he/she has created. The blackboard/whiteboard may be used for this purpose.
(5) The instructor may comment on the degree of originality displayed.
(6) Wrap up the activity by discussing the definition of creativity, levels of creativity, and facilitators and inhibitors influencing creativity.

Variations

(1) Participants may be asked to create words at random to represent anything that is important to them.
(2) Participants may be asked to create words belonging to different categories like flowers and games.

EXPERIENCING FREEWHEELING

Instructor guidelines

Objectives

This activity emphasizes ideation, providing participants an opportunity to let their minds freewheel in order to generate and work with wild and remote ideas. Experiencing the essence of uninhibited ideation is an important component of this exercise. Evaluating and elaborating on ideas and alternatives is also touched upon.

Time

Two hours and thirty minutes.

Material

(1) Art material including chart paper, glaze paper, crepe paper, paints, paint brushes, palettes, felt pens, crayons and color pencils.

(2) Stationery items including pencils, erasers, sharpeners, gum and scissors.

(3) Magazines for pictures (magazines covering a variety of topics such as business, cookery, travel and fashion should be included to provide a range of pictures).

(4) Classrooms/additional space with CD playing facilities so that participants may disperse and work on the task.

(5) Experiencing freewheeling worksheet (the number should be equal to the number of participants).

(6) Module 1 reflections sheet (the number should be equal to the number of participants).

(7) Module 1 reading handout (the number should be equal to the number of participants).

(8) Take-home assignment 1 (the number should be equal to the number of participants).

Procedure

(1) Participants may read the worksheet titled "Experiencing freewheeling" and complete the task assigned to them.

(2) Participants may be asked to present their work in front of the entire group.

(3) Module 1 reflections sheet may be completed and a discussion can be held to contrast the earlier case analysis task with the "Experiencing freewheeling" task.

(4) Wrap up the activity with a detailed discussion on creativity as a cognitive activity, linking it to the preceding activities of the workshop and to the rest of the course.

(5) Distribute the reading handout and take-home assignment 1.

Instructor may substitute the specific task indicated in the "Experiencing freewheeling" worksheet (that is, make the learning of accounting fun for management students) with any other activity, either related to the organization and its functions (in the case of organizational participants) or to the curriculum (in the case of business administration students), that is perceived by participants as particularly challenging.

EXPERIENCING FREEWHEELING

Worksheet

You must devise an activity/a strategy/a course plan/a pedagogy that will make the learning of accounting fun for management students. Allow your imagination to operate uninhibitedly and preserve all your ideas. Use the ideas that you have generated to produce an original and complete outcome. You may work on this on your own or in a group or rely essentially on yourself while engaging with the group occasionally. You may use any source of inspiration for this task including material brought by the instructor or other material (including observing the life around you) for which you may leave the room.

You may take 60 minutes to complete this task.

MODULE 1 REFLECTIONS SHEET

Take a few minutes to recollect and note down your thoughts, feelings and actions while working on the "Experiencing freewheeling" activity.

The following questions will give you some leads but are not meant to be exhaustive.

About today's workshop

(1) How did I proceed with the task at hand?
(2) How did I go about identifying and developing alternatives?
(3) Were there any factors influencing me?
(4) What were my thoughts about and what did they lead me to do?
(5) What were my feelings during various stages of the process—and how did they contribute to my task completion?
(6) What resources/supports (including intrapersonal ones) did I rely on during this exercise?
(7) Was I conscious of what I was doing/thinking/feeling during this time?

About myself

(1) Was I and were my thoughts/feelings/actions this time, different to what I was/what they were, during the case analysis?
(2) If so, what reasons would I attribute for this difference? Also, if so, would my orientation during the second activity have been more useful in helping find solutions to the case problem?
(3) Are there any areas that I need to work on/improve? If so, how do I plan to do so?

TAKE-HOME ASSIGNMENT 1

This assignment must be completed and submitted by the next workshop. You may use extra sheets as required.

(1) What are the most unusual uses you can think of for the following objects? List as many as you can, keeping in mind the principles of originality, fluency and flexibility.

Pencil

. . . .
. . . .

Envelope

....
....

Lock

....
....

(2) What responses strike you immediately when you are faced with the following stimulus? Try to keep your response as remote/unusual/uncommon as possible.

A difficult boss

....
....

A job transfer

....
....

(3) What idea emerges in your mind when you think of a concrete object and a sensory experience simultaneously, as in the instances given below?

A laptop and a sweet smell

....
....

A rabbit and a warm breeze

....
....

(4) Combine the following antitheses to come up with an original idea:

Hot and cold

....
....

Mars and Venus

....
....

Pleasure and torture

....
....

(5) Use the concept of elaboration to develop the following object into a creative/original/innovative final product.

Printer

....
....

File

....
....

(6) Take any product that you use regularly in your daily life but which you feel requires improvement in at least one aspect. Find innovative ways to improve it.

....
....
....

(7) Design a seal for yourself

....
....
....

(8) Invent a new game/sport

....
....
....

(9) Think of the last assignment/project you worked on. How many different ways did you define the task in? Which definition did you finally adopt? What were the ideas you started out with? What were the ideas you finally used? How could you improve this output further?

Had you adopted another definition, what difference would it have made to your ideational process and final output?

....
....
....

(10) Recall the wildest idea you have had in your life so far. Did you act on it? If yes, why and how? What does that tell you about yourself as a creative person? If no, why and how? What does that tell you about yourself as a creative person? What can you do to change this?

....
....
....

Module 2

Thinking Laterally

Lateral thinking, created and developed by Edward De Bono, involves the achievement of insight/breakthrough via the restructuring and rearrangement of information patterns. This restructuring and rearrangement, operationalized via various provocative techniques, results in the generation of alternatives, which lead to creative solutions (De Bono 1990).

According to De Bono (1990), information patterns are stable cognitive entities such as concepts, ideas, thoughts and images which exist in our minds and which provide a perspective that directs information processing/thinking/problem solving in a particular way. Generally, once information patterns are formed and appear to be useful in real situations, they are retained by the mind and repeatedly resorted to in similar and new situations, thereby acquiring an entrenched and rigid character. In other words, they operate on the lines of mindsets/schema. He postulates that though an information pattern provides a useful viewpoint, it is neither an absolute nor a unique way of looking at a situation/experience. Further, it may not even be the best way. Changing information patterns by restructuring the way in which information is arranged allows for alternative patterns to emerge, giving rise to new and sometimes more effective perspectives and insights.

Restructuring and rearrangement of information patterns is achieved through provocative techniques that are ideational, generative and exploratory in nature, resulting in the emergence of innumerable alternatives. These processes continue even after an appropriate alternative is found, in an attempt to find better, more appropriate ones. Lateral thinking never judges alternative patterns as right/wrong or correct/incorrect. Rather, it assumes each alternative to be one possibility in a range of possibilities that can be generated and that can serve as improvements over previous patterns. Keeping this in mind, lateral thinking is characterized by suspension of judgment and evaluation not only to allow for a free flow of alternatives but also to acknowledge the fact that new alternatives could be more effective than earlier ones. Lateral thinking thus stands in contrast to vertical thinking which entails moving purposefully and sequentially through a series of well-defined consecutive steps to a correct alternative (De Bono 1990).

De Bono (1990) has devised specific techniques of restructuring, rearrangement and provocation to aid alternative generation. In this module, we look at some of these techniques, categorizing them into two broad groups, namely, changing mindsets/schema and random stimulation.

CHANGING MINDSETS/SCHEMA

Mindsets/schema refer to cognitive frameworks that allow us to organize and process large amounts of information in an efficient manner. Serving as mental short cuts that help us reduce the effort we put in to understand the world around us and to preserve cognitive capacity, they simultaneously promote rigidity and distortions since information processing/thinking/problem solving are performed within their limits and boundaries (Baron and Byrne 2004). Challenging assumptions, identifying dominant ideas and changing entry points, and reversals are some of De Bono's (1990) strategies to overcome the adverse effects of mindsets/schema. They involve the generation of alternatives via rearrangement, restructuring and provocation derived from the situation/experience itself such that different aspects of the situation/experience that were not apparent earlier now emerge.

Challenging assumptions

Assumptions underlie information patterns, setting boundaries within which these patterns are perceived and used. Generally, when we re-structure information patterns, we fail to look at their assumptions but operate within these limits. Ironically, assumptions are self-imposed in order to facilitate information processing/thinking/problem solving. Apart from convenience, assumptions are maintained because of historical continuity and popular agreement, rather than because of their validity. De Bono (1990) proposes questioning the very basis of our patterns, maintaining that by examining assumptions, further restructuring and rearrangement of information patterns is possible, paving the way for insights and breakthroughs. The "why" game included in this module exemplifies this.

Identifying dominant ideas and changing entry points

When one is confronted with a situation/experience, a particular information pattern about it stands out and serves as the basis around which other patterns to deal with/look at the situation/experience are organized. De Bono (1990) terms this "the dominant idea." It is important to be aware of and to identify the dominant idea so that one is not frozen by it but instead is able to set it aside and look at the situation/experience from other angles. Picking out and setting aside the dominant idea allows one to escape from its influence, providing space for different entry points to view the situation/experience to emerge, and hence allowing for the generation of alternatives.

Using reversals

Reversals involve looking at the situation/experience from a completely opposite point of view. In other words, one takes a perspective in the direction that is completely contrary to the situation/experience. Through the restructuring and rearrangement of information patterns in a manner that is obviously wrong and ridiculous, one escapes from the absolute necessity of looking at the situation/experience in a standard way. Instead, restructuring and rearrangement provoke new perspectives, increasing the possibility of generating alternatives (De Bono 1990). There is no concept of true/correct reversal, and the process can take a variety of forms. The attempt is to rearrange information patterns provocatively and De Bono (1990) suggests that this could be done by taking things as they are and then turning them around, inside out, upside down, back to front, and so on. For instance, you can make water run uphill, instead of downhill, or your car leads you instead of you driving it (De Bono 1990).

Random stimulation

Random stimulation, which draws on associational thinking theory, involves juxtaposing the situation/experience with an unrelated external entity to stimulate and provoke restructuring, rearrangement and alternative generation. It is rooted in the belief that the association between unrelated/novel stimuli may change existing information patterns incrementally/radically, leading to insights and breakthroughs (De Bono 1990). Exposure and formal generation are two ways of developing random stimuli (De Bono 1990).

Exposure

Exposure includes accepting random inputs that appear within one's attention horizon, being open to the ideas of others and paying attention to ideas from completely different disciplines (also known as cross fertilization). Exposure is not the deliberate search for random stimulation—it occurs as one attends to stimuli that one encounters as part of one's activities (De Bono 1990).

Sensitivity to one's environment/context, henceforth termed as ecological sensitivity in this book, is relevant here. Cues picked up from the world around operate as exposure, serving as random stimulation.

Formal generation

De Bono (1990) maintains that the problem with exposure is that some amount of selectivity influences our attention, hampering the randomness of exposure. Hence if one truly wants to use random inputs, one has to generate them deliberately. De Bono (1990) suggests a formal process to produce random stimulation such as the use of a dictionary to provide a random word or the selection of a chapter or paper from a book or journal in a library. Similarly, pictures, poems, songs, objects, proverbs and analogies could all serve as random stimuli.

Suspension of judgment is a prerequisite for the aforementioned techniques. Following alternative generation, evaluation and elaboration are invoked to complete the process of finding a solution to the problem at hand.

ACTIVITY SEQUENCE

(1) Creating a Random Stimulus
(2) "Why" Game

(3) Changing Mindsets
(4) Random Stimuli as Provocation
(5) Engaging Forced Analogies and Proverbs

CREATING A RANDOM STIMULUS

Instructor guidelines

Objectives

The task to be assigned to participants involves their identifying/ creating a random stimulus which kick-starts their ideation at the beginning of the workshop and which is used as an associational mechanism to respond to a case situation during the course of the workshop. It is an appropriate warm up activity for a workshop on lateral thinking.

Time

Sixty minutes.

Material

(1) Art material including chart paper, glaze paper, crepe paper, paints, paint brushes, palettes, felt pens, crayons and color pencils.
(2) Stationery items including pencils, erasers, sharpeners, gum and scissors.
(3) Blank writing paper.

Procedure

(1) Participants are asked to move anywhere in the vicinity and respond to any entity that hits any one of their senses. They must then write a story or poem/compose a song/draw or paint or make a collage/use any other medium of communication to depict their experience. They must return back to the class room after 45 minutes with their creation.
(2) Some participants may be called upon to share their creation with the group.
(3) Participants are instructed to retain their creation during the workshop.

"WHY" GAME

Instructor guidelines

Objectives

This activity demonstrates one way of challenging assumptions which form part of the mindsets/schema that influence our cognitive processes.

Time

Thirty minutes.

Material

(1) Large plastic/cardboard container.
(2) Small strips of colored paper (the number should be equal to the number of participants).
(3) "Why" game debrief note (the number should be equal to the number of participants).

Procedure

(1) Ask half the participants to wait outside the room.
(2) Distribute the strips of paper to the remaining half and ask them to write down a question whose answer they have always been looking for but have never been able to find. They must also write their name below the question and then deposit the same in the container. Once this has been completed, they may wait outside.
(3) Bring the first group of participants back into the room. Each of them must pick a strip of paper from the container and find the person whose name is on it. Then they must spend 10 minutes with that person in a dyadic encounter initiated via the question on the slip and followed up with "why" and variations of "why" (such as why do you say so, why do you think like that, what is the reason for that, and so on) as a rejoinder for every response their partner makes.

(4) Once this part of the exercise has been completed, ask participants to share their experiences and learnings.

(5) Introduce the concept of lateral thinking and of changing mindsets/schema. Indicate the position of the "why" game in this.

(6) Distribute the debrief sheet and give them some time to read it.

"WHY" GAME

Debrief

Assumptions underlie information patterns (that is, stable cognitive entities such as concepts, ideas, thoughts and images which exist in our minds and which provide a perspective that directs information processing/thinking/problem solving in a particular way), setting boundaries within which these patterns are perceived and used. Generally, when we restructure information patterns, we fail to look at their assumptions but operate within these limits. De Bono (1990) proposes questioning the very basis of our patterns, maintaining that by examining assumptions, further restructuring and rearrangement of information patterns is possible, paving the way for insights and breakthroughs. The "why" technique is a means of practicing the challenging of assumptions. Even if one knows the answer to "why" or one provides a familiar/acceptable answer to "why", one continues to question in order to realize that what is familiar/acceptable/taken for granted need not be sacrosanct. Instead of being comforted with explanations that we can accept and be satisfied with, the lateral use of "why" is the opposite. The intention is to create discomfort with any explanation such that the discomfort leads one to look at things in a different way and hence increases the possibility of restructuring and rearranging the existing information pattern (De Bono 1990).

While one may not have the time to challenge every assumption on every occasion, it is important to realize that nothing is sacred. The idea is not to sow so much doubt that one becomes indecisive nor is it to nullify the relevance of assumptions as cognitive aids—rather it is to highlight that one should not be imprisoned by assumptions (De Bono 1990).

CHANGING MINDSETS

Instructor guidelines

Objectives

A case is used to show participants the limitations that emerge from mindsets/schema. That dominant ideas arise in response to a problem/situation is highlighted. That setting aside the dominant idea and changing the entry point allow for a more holistic perspective of the problem/situation is illustrated. The role of reversal as a tool for restructuring/rearrangement/provocation is demonstrated.

Time

Eighty minutes.

Material

(1) Changing mindsets worksheet I (the number of copies must match the number of participants).
(2) Changing mindsets worksheet II (the number of copies must match the number of participants).
(3) Blackboard with chalk/whiteboard with markers.

Procedure

(1) Participants are asked to work on "Changing mindsets" worksheet I for about 30 minutes.
(2) Some participants are asked to share their responses.
(3) Wrap up this part of the activity by discussing how setting aside the dominant idea and changing the entry point provide a more comprehensive perspective of the problem/situation, broadening the scope of alternative generation.
(4) Move on to "Changing mindsets" worksheet II and let participants work on this for 10 minutes.
(5) Ask some participants to share their responses.
(6) Explain the relevance of reversal as a means of restructuring, rearrangement and provocation.
(7) Work in the group using reversal as a tool to generate alternatives for the case problem.

CHANGING MINDSETS

Worksheet I

Read the case below and answer the questions that follow. You may take 30 minutes to complete this task.

Hope Hospital

Hope Hospital, a general hospital located in an East Indian town, usually works beyond its capacity to meet the needs of the local community in which it is situated. The hospital is staffed by specialized consultant doctors, full-time resident doctors, nurses and ward assistants, in addition to administrative personnel. Hope Hospital continues to follow personnel policies and procedures laid down at its inception 20 years ago even though these no longer suit the current trends. Everyone working at the hospital realizes the outdatedness of these policies and procedures while also acknowledging that actual practices operate completely differently. Yet, no one has shown any initiative to make any changes.

Nurses, who have three groups comprising staff nurses, paraprofessional nurses and student nurses, are at the core of in-patient care, being the critical point of round-the-clock contact with patients. The performance of the nursing staff is therefore crucial. Yet the hospital's personnel policies have begun to create severe conflict among nursing staff, adversely affecting the overall hospital functioning. The qualifications, job descriptions and benefits of each group are laid out in personnel documents. Staff nurses must be graduates in nursing, have maximum responsibility for patient care including being able to modify treatment regimens/perform minor invasive procedures with medical personnel's approval and administer injections, liaison with medical personnel, and supervise paraprofessional and student nurses. In addition to receiving the highest pay scales among the nursing staff, the staff nurses enjoy overtime, medical leave, casual leave, earned leave and retirement benefits. Paraprofessional nurses, who should have cleared a certificate course in nursing to qualify for the job, are expected to carry out the instructions of the staff nurses in the provision of patient care. They are not permitted to perform any procedures or administer injections. Besides their salaries, paraprofessional nurses receive two weeks of leave per year and enjoy overtime and retirement benefits only after five years on the job. Student nurses, who are working towards a degree or a certificate, are supervised by staff nurses. The tasks that they engage in depend on the course they are enrolled for. That is, while both groups of student nurses execute patient care, only degree students are exposed to administering injections, performing invasive procedures and planning treatment regimens. Student nurses do not receive any remuneration/benefits for their services, which are considered to be part of their training process.

Quite contrary to the job description laid down in the personnel handbooks, in reality, paraprofessional nurses perform the same tasks and roles as staff nurses, a development that has got institutionalized over the years with the growing demands placed on the hospital. Staff nurses are quite happy to receive the support of their paraprofessional colleagues as they know fully well that they would never be able to manage without it. Thus, paraprofessional nurses modify medical regimens, administer injections and perform minor invasive procedures, in addition to their specified responsibilities. Indeed, the tasks and roles of both paraprofessional and staff nurses completely overlap such that no one questions who is performing which role, but takes it for granted that either group would be able to do so competently. This is important especially because with the high volumes at the hospital, there never seems to be enough of time or help.

Yet, over a period of time, the paraprofessional nurses have been voicing their concern over the difference in benefits between them and the staff nurses. They believe that when they are working as hard as, and at the same level as, the staff nurses, their returns should also be equalized. The paraprofessional nurses have met up with the administration of Hope Hospital several times in order to redress their grievances but they have met with little success. Apart from lending a patient ear to listen to the paraprofessional nurses' problems, the administration maintains that the policies and procedures are sacrosanct and cannot be changed.

Reacting to the impasse and the apparent lack of solutions, paraprofessional nurses have recently decided that they will stick to tasks and roles specified for them in the personnel document. Operating in this fashion has reduced the support that staff nurses receive. But in spite of the upsurge in work pressure which they now have to deal with single-handedly, staff nurses refuse to support the paraprofessional nurses' point of view. In their opinion, paraprofessional nurses lack the technical qualification that they have and hence should not receive the same benefits as they do. Hostile feelings have now emerged between the two groups making it difficult for them to work together. Not only has the morale dropped among nursing staff but the quality of patient care has also been adversely affected.

(1) What is the issue(s) that immediately comes to your mind when you read this case?

....

....

....

(2) Putting aside the initial issue(s) that leapt to your mind, list other issues that strike you.

....

....

....

CHANGING MINDSETS

Worksheet II

Reversals involve looking at the situation/experience from a completely opposite point of view. In other words, one takes a perspective in the direction that is completely contrary to the situation/experience. Through the restructuring and rearrangement of information patterns in a manner that is obviously wrong and ridiculous, one escapes from the absolute necessity of looking at the situation/experience in a standard way. Instead, restructuring and rearrangement via reversal provoke new perspectives, increasing the possibility of generating alternatives (De Bono 1990). There is no concept of true/correct reversal, and the process can take a variety of forms. The attempt is to rearrange information patterns provocatively and De Bono (1990) suggests that this could be done by taking things as they are and then turning them around, inside out, upside down, back to front, and so on. For instance, you can make water run uphill, instead of downhill, or your car leads you instead of you driving it (De Bono 1990).

Your task

Looking at the issues you have identified in the case, what kind of reversals can you come up with? You may take 10 minutes to complete this task.

RANDOM STIMULI AS PROVOCATION

Instructor guidelines

Objectives

Participants must use the random stimulus they created in the beginning of the workshop as a tool to generate alternatives to solve the case. Through this activity, participants learn about the role of random stimulation as a source of restructuring, rearrangement and provocation.

Time

Ninety minutes.

Material

(1) Random stimuli as provocation worksheet (the number of copies must match the number of participants).
(2) Blackboard with chalk/whiteboard with markers.

Procedure

(1) Participants now move on to "Random stimuli as provocation", using the worksheet provided. They must complete the task in 30 minutes.
(2) Ask participants to share their responses. Provide feedback on their work.

(3) Explain the role of random stimulation in lateral thinking, how random stimuli are created, the link between random stimulation and associational thinking theories, and the role of evaluation/elaboration/convergent thinking in the creativity process.

RANDOM STIMULI AS PROVOCATION

Worksheet

Use the random stimulus you created earlier during the workshop as a means of restructuring, rearrangement and provocation to generate alternatives for the case problem(s). It does not matter if these alternatives are wild/unfeasible—allow your random stimulus to provoke your thought processes and to let your mind freewheel in order to identify original and innovative alternatives.

You may take 30 minutes to complete this task.

ENGAGING FORCED ANALOGIES AND PROVERBS

Instructor guidelines

Objectives

Forced analogies operate in the same manner as random stimulation. This activity is designed to provide participants with further practice in the use of random stimulation. This activity will also be used to initiate the use of proverbs as a means of random stimulation (the completion of this part is included in the take-home assignment).

Time

Ninety minutes.

Material

(1) Small strips of blank colored paper (four times in number as the number of participants).
(2) Two large plastic/cardboard containers.

(3) Engaging forced analogies worksheet (the number of copies must match the number of participants).

(4) Small strips of colored paper on which a forced analogy is printed (these should be as many as the number of participants and should be kept in a plastic/cardboard container).

(5) Small strips of colored paper on which a proverb is printed (these should be as many as the number of participants and should be kept in a plastic/cardboard container).

(6) Module 2 reflections sheet (the number of copies must match the number of participants).

(7) Take-home assignment 2 (the number of copies must match the number of participants).

(8) Module 2 reading handout (the number of copies must match the number of participants).

Please note that examples of forced analogies and proverbs are provided in this book.

Procedure

(1) Distribute the blank strips of paper and ask participants to write down at least one organizational related problem (at any level of analysis, namely, individual, group or organizational levels) and at least one problem relating to any other aspect of business. Participants may write more than one problem for each category.

Please note that some problems are provided in this book and may be used by the instructor in lieu of asking participants to generate problems. Alternatively, the instructor may use problems generated by him/her.

(2) Participants must then put the organization-related problem into one container and the business-related problem into the other container.

(3) Participants are next asked to read the "Engaging forced analogies" worksheet. After picking up a forced analogy from the container on the instructor's table, they must complete steps 2 and 3 of the worksheet.

(4) Participants then pick up an organization-related problem from the relevant container on the instructor's table and find solutions to it following step 4 of the worksheet.

(5) Participants are asked to share their responses and the instructor provides feedback on the same.

(6) Following completion of the forced analogy task, participants are asked to pick up proverbs and business-related problems in order to complete their take-home assignment.

(7) Wrap up the workshop by going over the basics of lateral thinking.

(8) Participants are asked to fill out the Module 2 reflections sheet.

(9) Module 2 reading handout and take-home assignment 2 may be distributed at this stage.

ENGAGING FORCED ANALOGIES

Worksheet

Analogies operate as random stimuli that juxtapose the problem/situation with an unrelated external entity to stimulate and provoke restructuring, rearrangement and alternative generation. It is rooted in the belief that the association between unrelated/novel stimuli may change existing information patterns incrementally/radically, leading to insights and breakthroughs.

Using analogies as random stimuli involves the following steps:

Step 1: Take a forced analogy

Example: Organization as angel

Step 2: List the attributes of angel

Example: (1) Purity and gentleness
(2) Ability to fly
(3) Harbinger of joy and peace
(4) Means to divinity

Step 3: Link angel attributes with organization

Example: (1) The offerings of the organization should embody purity and gentleness.
(2) Becoming and staying market leaders.
(3) The organization spreads joy and peace to internal and external stakeholders.
(4) The organization never loses sight of its goals and values.

Step 4: Generate solutions using the ideas from Step 3. These solutions may be wild and unfeasible and you may have to go through several iterations (where you may merge/mutate/splice, and so on) to make them practical.

Your task

(1) Each of you must pick a card from the pile on the table.
(2) List out the attributes of the analogical entity.
(3) Use the attributes listed in step 2 to develop ideas (however remote and exotic) about an organization.
(4) Pick out a problem from the container on the table and find solutions for it with the help of ideas from step 3.

Please note that proverbs which are included in your take-home exercise operate in a similar manner. Instructions for this will be provided to you following completion of the "Engaging forced analogies" exercise.

EXAMPLES OF FORCED ANALOGIES

(1) Organization as locker
(2) Organization as socks
(3) Organization as lotus
(4) Organization as feather
(5) Organization as almond
(6) Organization as jeans
(7) Organization as comet

(8) Organization as brick
(9) Organization as bulb
(10) Organization as thread
(11) Organization as bell
(12) Organization as traffic signal
(13) Organization as rope
(14) Organization as lipstick
(15) Organization as sieve
(16) Organization as saucer
(17) Organization as pedal
(18) Organization as oven
(19) Organization as house
(20) Organization as baby
(21) Organization as jelly
(22) Organization as printer
(23) Organization as bottle
(24) Organization as flag
(25) Organization as song
(26) Organization as film
(27) Organization as tank
(28) Organization as pen
(29) Organization as bandage
(30) Organization as forceps
(31) Organization as cradle
(32) Organization as pastry
(33) Organization as winter
(34) Organization as rain
(35) Organization as jacket

EXAMPLES OF PROVERBS

(1) The apple never falls far from the tree.
(2) A chain is no stronger than its weakest link.
(3) Discretion is the better part of valor.
(4) Everyone speaks well of the bridge which carries him over.
(5) Example is better than precept.

(6) The exception proves the rule.
(7) Give a dog a bad name and hang him.
(8) Good fences make good neighbors.
(9) Great oaks from little acorns grow.
(10) Happy is the country which has no history.
(11) Imitation is the sincerest form of flattery.
(12) It is a poor heart that never rejoices.
(13) Lend your money and lose your friend.
(14) A little knowledge is a dangerous thing.
(15) Little things please little minds.
(16) Man is the measure of all things.
(17) Many are called but few are chosen.
(18) Never let the sun go down on your anger.
(19) Old habits die hard.
(20) Politics makes strange bedfellows.
(21) A rising tide lifts all boats.
(22) The sharper the storm, the sooner it's over.
(23) Still waters run deep.
(24) There's no place like home.
(25) Thrift is a great revenue.
(26) The tree is known by its fruit.
(27) Truth is stranger than fiction.
(28) Virtue is its own reward.
(29) A woman's work is never done.
(30) To be content with little is hard; to be content with much is impossible.

EXAMPLES OF PROBLEMS

(1) How can you help people in an organization reconcile conflicting individual and collective goals?
(2) How should organizations build up team spirit while facilitating individual space?
(3) What can an organization do to ensure employee commitment in the light of the current psychological contract?

(4) How can a double-loop learning system be incorporated into an organization at all levels?

(5) How can the Human Resources (HR) department ensure that it plays a more strategic/core role in organizational functioning?

(6) What is the best way for an organization to handle defensive routines/behaviors that blinker it?

(7) Leaders and managers tend to rely on intuition when taking decisions in uncertain and time-bound contexts, and this results in faulty decisions and outcomes. How can this be avoided?

(8) How can you eliminate latent conflict from an organization?

(9) What is the best way of preparing employees for change and pre-empting resistance?

(10) How can the importance of corporate social responsibility (CSR) be stressed to internal stakeholders in an organization?

(11) How can organizations treat whistle-blowers with dignity?

(12) What can be done to prevent the misuse of power in an organization?

(13) What can be done to contain attrition in the Information Technology (IT)/Information Technology Enabled Services (ITES) sector?

(14) What kind of indicators can be developed to assess organization citizenship behavior?

(15) How can employee assistance programs support employees without building up a stigma around them for being in need of help?

(16) What mechanism(s) can an organization employ to maintain healthy levels of conflict which promote optimal functioning and performance?

(17) How can the resilience of employees be developed so that organizational crises do not induce individual dysfunction?

(18) How would you ensure that the organization has both conformity and individuality simultaneously?

(19) How would you attempt to achieve optimal decision making in an organization?

(20) What measures would you take to develop constructive criticism mechanisms within your team?

(21)   How would you prevent sexual harassment at your workplace?
(22)   How would you ensure that the move to maintain creativity within your organization does not lead to chaos?
(23)   What is the best way for an organization to capitalize on diversity and become truly multicultural?

MODULE 2 REFLECTIONS SHEET

Take a few minutes to recollect and note down your thoughts, feelings and actions on completion of today's workshop. While the questions below will give you some leads, they are not meant to be exhaustive.

About today's workshop

(1)   Was this problem solving different to what I usually do? In what way?
(2)   Was this different to the exercises I did last week? If yes, how and why? How do I feel about adopting such a problem solving style?
(3)   How did I perform? Were there any factors like thoughts and feelings influencing me during the problem solving process—and how did they contribute to my task completion? What resources/supports (including intrapersonal ones) did I rely on during today's exercises? Was I conscious of what I was doing/thinking/feeling during this time?
(4)   What changes do I see in myself? Anything that I need to work on?

About myself

(1)   Am I more aware of my cognitive processes as well as aspects of myself and how these affect my ability to think creatively?
(2)   What changes have I observed in myself/my way of thinking since Workshop 1?
(3)   Are these changes influencing my everyday life/activities/thinking?
(4)   Which areas require further strengthening?

(5) In what way does Workshop 2 take this process forward?

(6) Are there any areas that I need to work on/improve? If so, how do I plan to do so?

TAKE-HOME ASSIGNMENT 2

This assignment must be completed and submitted by the next workshop. You may use extra sheets as required.

(1) As part of your ecological sensitivity:

Recall as many different tastes that you have come across over the course of your life.

. . . .

. . . .

. . . .

List the different kinds of buildings you saw on your way home from the office/your last trip outside the institute campus.

. . . .

. . . .

. . . .

(2) Keeping in mind the relevance of changing mindsets, what are the different ways in which you can look at the following situations:

Economic liberalization is deepening the inequity in Indian society. It is only a matter of time before a backlash surfaces.

. . . .

. . . .

. . . .

The number of educated unemployed is falling drastically, thanks to the outsourcing boom.

. . . .

. . . .

. . . .

(3) What outcome do you envisage from the combination of the following two completely unrelated entities? Keep your response as original as possible.

A brick and a wine glass

....

....

....

A horse and a submarine

....

....

....

(4) Design a logo and a letterhead for your organization/institute.

....

....

....

(5) Describe your organization/institute in verse.

....

....

....

(6) As was highlighted during the last workshop, proverbs can be used as random stimuli for restructuring, rearrangement and provocation in order to generate alternatives, as shown in the following example.

Step 1: Note down whatever ideas/associations come to your mind on seeing the following proverb. Do not hesitate to include outlandish and weird ideas/associations.

Proverb: The pen is mightier than the sword.

Ideas/associations:

(1) As contrary things attract each other, the pen and the sword fit together and symbolize balance.

(2) Cognition is the best way to inculcate discipline.

(3) Metals can be fashioned in innumerable ways.

(4) Pen and sword are ideal marriage partners.

(5) Word bombs drive humanity.

Step 2: Derive wild/remote/unfeasible alternatives from the ideas/associations to solve the problem at hand. Refine these alternatives to make them into practical and workable solutions.

Your task

Using the proverb you picked out during workshop 2, note down ideas/associations that strike you. Now look at the problem you picked during workshop 2 and use the ideas/associations you just identified to find alternatives and solutions.

(7) Read the case and answer the questions that follow:

Sri Ganesh Autospares

Sri Ganesh Autospares, a medium-sized enterprise located in south India, produces spare parts for light motor vehicles. Owned and managed by the Rangarajan family who maintained a tight control over all aspects of organizational functioning, Sri Ganesh's focus was on production and sales with some emphasis on new product development. Over its 20-year existence, the company, known for its quality products, has developed a large client base including automobile manufacturers and service stations, particularly those based in the region. The company has distinguished itself via its production efficiency, product quality, salesmanship and reliable delivery processes, and periodic product innovations that enhanced vehicular efficiency and performance. Sri Ganesh clearly enjoyed a large and comfortable market share, facing very little competition to its position.

The opening up of the Indian economy completely altered the face of the automobile spare parts sector. Foreign automobile manufacturers not only had their own spare parts divisions/subsidiaries, there were also imports and foreign players from the automobile spare parts industry itself. The management of Sri Ganesh grew apprehensive that market share would fall rapidly, and to take care of that eventuality, they introduced three new elements, namely, higher targets for sales, innovative products for research and development, and quality controls and increased output (faster turnaround and increased quantity) for production. While these targets were assigned to the respective functional departments, in terms of their actual achievement, it was the people at the lower levels of the organizational hierarchy who had to deliver. While incentives were planned for those who met the requirements and penalties for those who failed to do so, no financial/resource allocations were made to facilitate the achievement of the new targets. Moreover, performance assessment and reward distribution were to be conducted on an individual basis, even in cases where task completion was team-based.

In the period immediately after the new targets were introduced, Sri Ganesh's employees responded with great enthusiasm. They believed that the future of the organization rested on their endeavors and hence extended themselves to meet organizational expectations. After the initial high in terms of effort and performance, employees grew disgruntled. The pressure which resulted from such targets was enormous and led to considerable physical and mental strain on employees as well as high degrees of interpersonal rivalry and competition, given the individual basis for evaluation and rewards. The absence of sufficient resources to facilitate performance made task completion almost insurmountable. Not only did product output in terms of quality and quantity plunge, the supply/delivery process to clients was also no longer dependable as it had been in the past. Clients and suppliers spoke of the aggressive and high-handed approach of Sri Ganesh employees, which was a result of the pressures to meet targets. It was not surprising that the organizational climate at Sri Ganesh displayed almost complete disintegration and the organization also began to lose market share rapidly.

The presence of foreign automakers/spare parts manufacturers opened up innumerable opportunities in the job market. The top and middle management of Sri Ganesh who enjoyed employability and mobility options, began to leave to join these organizations who paid more and whose brands had global presence and visibility. Apart from cutting into the talent pool and the competence of Sri Ganesh, this development resulted in competitors getting insight into Sri Ganesh's functioning, strategies and future plans. Despite the deepening vulnerability of the company, the owners and the Board of Sri Ganesh decided to maintain their current strategy, considering it to be correct in the long run.

(a) What is the issue(s) that immediately comes to your mind when you read this case?

. . . .

. . . .

. . . .

(b) Putting aside the initial issue(s) that leapt to your mind, list other issues that strike you.

. . . .

. . . .

. . . .

(c) Looking at the issues you have identified, what kind of reversals can you come up with?

. . . .

. . . .

. . . .

(d) What solutions do the reversals suggest? (Allow your mind to freewheel and then refine).

. . . .

. . . .

. . . .

(8) List the innovations that your organization/institute devised in the last one year. Can these be categorized in any way? How would you rate them in terms of originality? Can you improve them further?

....
....
....

(9) Consider your life. List all the things that you want to do/ achieve, including those that are realistic and unrealistic as well as those that are safe and risky. Assign labels of realistic, unrealistic, risky or safe to each of them, as appropriate. Think of ways in which you can actualize your unrealistic/risky ideas.

....
....
....

(10) Are there any areas of your career in which you need to be creative?

....
....
....

Module 3

Relayering

INTRODUCTORY NOTE

Relayering involves developing innovative solutions/achieving creative breakthroughs by exploring the aspects/constituents/ components of the problem. Relayering includes a variety of techniques which fall into two broad categories: delving techniques and associational techniques. Delving techniques include those that break down the problem into its components and make alternative suggestions for each component. Potential solutions emerge from combinations of alternatives. Examples of delving techniques include morphological analysis (Zwicky 1948), checklists (Osborn 1953), sequence attribution matrices (Proctor 1999) and attribute listing (Crawford 1954). Associational techniques encompass those which rely on additional stimulation that either derives from the components or gives rise to components. Potential solutions are triggered by additional stimulation. Force fitting triggers (Proctor 1999), heuristic ideation (Tauber 1972) and componential detailing (Wakin, cited in Proctor 1999) illustrate associational techniques.

In this module, we consider the delving techniques of question banks (derived from checklists) and morphological analysis and the associational techniques of force fitting triggers and componential detailing.

Question banks

The idea of using questions to stimulate divergent thinking is credited to Alex Osborn (1953). Questioning allows for a detailed examination of the problem at hand because it leads one to examine the problem from different angles. In the process of asking questions, alternatives concomitantly emerge as one attempts to provide multiple answers to the questions.

The types of questions that could be asked are innumerable and those listed below are only meant to be illustrative:

Why?	Who?	Where?	What?
When?	How?	How much?	How many?
Change?	Minimize?	How far?	How long?
Modify?	Rearrange?	Substitute?	Reverse?
Enlarge?	Combine?	Whom?	Add?
Subtract?	Remove?	Adapt?	Include?
Exclude?	Simplify?	Complicate?	Whether?
Which?			

The ideas that emerge from the questions/answers to the questions provide possible solutions/leads for possible solutions. It is possible that one may combine the ideas from several questions/answers to questions in the search for solutions.

Question banks can be used as individual or group activities. As a group activity, members may work individually and then pool their ideas together to find a solution or they may work collectively. If members are working individually, it is important that they may also be able to think of unusual alternatives. It is important that the group climate be one of suspended judgment so that uninhibited ideation is facilitated. The presence of a leader is recommended to facilitate the group process.

Morphological analysis

Morphological analysis, developed by Swiss astronomer Fritz Zwicky (1948), facilitates the generation of a large pool of ideas. It involves listing the existing attribute(s) of each dimension of the problem and providing as many alternatives as possible (including wild and off-beat ones) for each attribute. Combinations of the alternatives generated can lead to new ideas and creative insights. Undoubtedly, the more remote/wilder the alternatives, the more novel/unique are the outcomes. While some outcomes may be impractical, other practical ones that may have earlier been overlooked, have an opportunity to emerge (Khandwalla 2004). Moreover, unusual/impractical combinations can be considered as they can throw up further ideas that are worth pursuing (Proctor 1999). Morphological analysis can be used to generate ideas for products and processes, and it works best when the problem under consideration has two or three dimensions (Proctor 1999).

Morphological analysis may be used by an individual or a group. In the group context, it is important that group members agree on the dimensions that they would like to consider prior to listing attributes and generating alternatives. Once consensus has been reached, group members could work individually or collectively on identifying attributes and providing ideas, both of which can be collated either when they have completed this phase of the activity or after a specified period of time has elapsed. The ideas that emerge from the alternatives suggested for each feature provide possible solutions/leads for possible solutions. It is possible that one may combine the ideas from several alternatives in the search for solutions. The facilitative role of a leader would greatly enhance the group process.

Force fitting triggers

As an associational relayering technique, force fitting triggers serve as additional stimulation that give rise to components/attributes which in turn lead to solutions/potential solutions.

Force fitting triggers could be either pictures or words. The attributes triggered by the picture or the word are used as ideas to develop solutions for problems (Proctor 1999).

When one is confronted with a problem, one puts aside the problem from one's mind temporarily. Force fitting triggers are picked up at random: usually three force fitting triggers (three picture cards/three word cards/one word card + two picture cards/one picture card + two word cards) are selected. All the attributes that immediately strike one's mind on seeing the trigger cards are listed—this is done separately for each trigger card. Once this list is completed, a combination of one attribute from each card is taken and used as a stimulus for ideas which are then considered in the problem solving process. Numerous rounds of combinations may be resorted to such that a large pool of potential ideas is developed.

Force fitting triggers operate on the principles of associational thinking where the attempt is to come up with a creative solution triggered by ideas that emerge from the combination of random stimuli that are unrelated to the problem at hand.

Force fitting triggers could work as an individual or group activity. As a group activity, each member of the group could individually generate lists of attributes associated with their respective three randomly selected trigger cards. Individual members could come up with solutions based on numerous combinations of attributes from their three lists and these could be shared with and discussed by the larger group. Alternatively, a list of one combination of three attributes can be collected from each group member. This list can be either jointly used by the group to come up with solutions or it could be used by individual members to come up with solutions that are then discussed within the group. Another variation is that the group as a whole could react to three trigger cards, compiling a list of attributes associated with each trigger card. They could then combine one attribute from each list and develop ideas for potential solutions.

Componential detailing

This is a group relayering associational technique in which components trigger additional stimulation which is used for ideation and problem solving. Suggested by Wakin (cited in Proctor 1999), componential detailing entails that the group collectively analyzes the problem at hand to identify its different components. The group divides into sub-groups and different problem components are allocated to different sub-groups for further work. Each sub-group develops a picture of their component, including as many details as possible. This picture indicates how the sub-group views the component and could represent their conceptualization of the problem/wild ideas that come to their mind. The pictures developed by all the sub-groups are collected and displayed together as a single collage, in an order decided by the group.

The group as a whole reviews the collage for ideas which serve as stimuli for solutions rather than solutions in themselves. These ideas, which are derived from the collage as a whole or from parts of it, could be used as they are or they could be joined together or they could be further developed. They could inspire even more ideas. Ideas may start out as wild and unfeasible, and hence they may have to undergo several refinements before they are amenable to application.

ACTIVITY SEQUENCE

(1) Sensory Monitor
(2) Force Fitting Triggers
(3) Question Banks
(4) Morphological Analysis
(5) Componential Detailing

SENSORY MONITOR

Instructor guidelines

Objectives

To get participants started into the workshop with an opportunity to experience ecological sensitivity, a part of the exposure form of random stimulation.

Time

Forty five minutes.

Procedure

(1) Once all the participants have assembled, the instructor may engage them in a discussion using the questions listed below. Each question may be asked to two or three participants. The instructor may devise further questions on these lines:

(*a*) How many colors did you observe from the time you woke up this morning?
(*b*) How many sounds did you hear?
(*c*) How many objects did you touch?
(*d*) Which were the birds you saw?
(*e*) Did you come across anything in the course of last week which baffled you? What was this? What are your thoughts about it?
(*f*) Has there been anything that you have come across over the course of your life that has puzzled you—what was it? Did you ever attempt to look for answers to it?

Questions related to the office and the institute may be included.

(2) The instructor can wrap up the activity by referring to the concept of ecological sensitivity, its link with ideation and creativity, associational thinking theory and lateral thinking.

FORCE FITTING TRIGGERS

Instructor guidelines

Objectives

This exercise is designed for participants to appreciate force fitting triggers as ideating tools and to introduce the concept of relayering.

Time

Forty five minutes.

Material

(1) Force fitting trigger cards (either picture cards and/or word cards may be used—a few examples of these are included in this book as a reference point. The instructor may develop more triggers on these lines, ensuring that they cover a range of themes/categories).

(2) Force fitting triggers worksheet (the number of copies must match the number of participants).

Procedure

(1) Participants may pick up three force fitting trigger cards each. The specifics of this can be decided by the instructor—that is, they can pick up either two picture cards and one word card or three picture cards or one picture card and two word cards, and so on.

(2) They should write down in about 10 minutes all the attributes that immediately come to their mind on seeing the trigger cards. The "force fitting triggers" worksheet may be used for this.

(3) Participants may be asked to share their triggers and attributes.

(4) The instructor must ask them to retain these attributes and use them in the take-home assignment. The instructor explains how these are to be used in the assignment.

(5) The activity is wrapped up by elaborating on the concept of relayering.

FORCE FITTING TRIGGERS

Worksheet

Trigger Card	Attributes
Trigger Card 1	
Trigger Card 2	
Trigger Card 3	

Keep this sheet with you and use the attributes as part of your take-home assignment.

Please return the trigger cards once you have completed noting down your ideas.

EXAMPLE OF PICTURE FORCE FITTING TRIGGER 1

Picture taken by Professor Ernesto Noronha, Indian Institute of Management, Ahmedabad.

EXAMPLE OF PICTURE FORCE FITTING TRIGGER 2

Picture taken by Professor Ernesto Noronha, Indian Institute of Management, Ahmedabad.

Picture taken by Professor Ernesto Noronha, Indian Institute of Management, Ahmedabad.

EXAMPLE OF PICTURE FORCE FITTING TRIGGER 4

Picture taken by Professor Ernesto Noronha, Indian Institute of Management, Ahmedabad.

Picture taken by Professor Ernesto Noronha, Indian Institute of Management, Ahmedabad.

EXAMPLE OF WORD FORCE FITTING TRIGGER 1

Shark

EXAMPLE OF WORD FORCE FITTING TRIGGER 2

Cake

EXAMPLE OF WORD FORCE FITTING TRIGGER 3

Knee

EXAMPLE OF WORD FORCE FITTING TRIGGER 4

Joy

EXAMPLE OF WORD FORCE FITTING TRIGGER 5

Tennis

QUESTION BANKS

Instructor guidelines

Objectives

To help participants understand how questions can stimulate ideation.

Time

Forty five minutes.

Material

Question bank worksheet (the number of copies must match the number of participants).

Procedure

(1) Explain, with the help of an example, how questions may be used to facilitate ideation and creativity.
(2) Participants may then complete the task assigned on the worksheet in 10 minutes.
(3) Participants may be asked to share their responses, and feedback may be provided.

QUESTION BANKS

Worksheet

The idea of using questions to stimulate ideation is credited to Alex Osborn (1953). Questioning allows for a detailed examination of the problem at hand because it leads one to examine the problem from different angles. In the process of asking questions, alternatives concomitantly emerge as one attempts to provide multiple answers to the questions.

The types of questions that could be asked are innumerable and those listed below are only meant to be illustrative:

Why?	Who?	Where?	What?
When?	How?	How much?	How many?
Change?	Minimize?	How far?	How long?
Modify?	Rearrange?	Substitute?	Reverse?
Enlarge?	Combine?	Whom?	Add?
Subtract?	Remove?	Adapt?	Include?
Exclude?	Simplify?	Complicate?	Whether?
Which?			

For example: Devise an innovative photocopier machine using a question bank.

(1) **For whom:** For people of all ages, including young children and senior citizens.

(2) **Where:** Offices, homes, supermarkets, buses, cars, trains, parks, zoos.

(3) **How:** Operate it on batteries, mechanically, with solar energy, with wind energy.

(4) **Minimize:** Make it portable, make it small enough to fit into a lady's purse.

(5) **Adapt:** Let it be fitted with a computer/laptop.

(6) **Maximize:** Make it a single office utilities entity with phone, fax, computer, printer, and so on.

(7) **Combine:** Combine with collapsible stands so that it can be made to stand independently, with flaps so that it opens out into a table.

The ideas that emerge from the questions/answers to the questions provide possible solutions/leads for possible solutions. It is possible that one may combine the ideas from several questions/answers to questions in the search for solutions.

Your task

Create a new type of filing cabinet, using questions as an ideating tool. You may ask any questions beyond those included above (10 minutes).

MORPHOLOGICAL ANALYSIS

Instructor guidelines

Objectives

To help participants understand how identifying and changing the attributes of each dimension of a problem stimulates ideation.

Time

Forty five minutes.

Material

Morphological analysis worksheet (the number of copies must match the number of participants).

Procedure

(1) Explain, with the help of an example, how the morphological analysis process is to be operationalized and how it contributes to ideation and creativity.

(2) Participants complete the task assigned on the worksheet in 10 minutes.

(3) Participants may be asked to share their responses, and feedback may be provided.

MORPHOLOGICAL ANALYSIS

Worksheet

Morphological analysis, developed by Swiss astronomer Fritz Zwicky (1948), facilitates the generation of a large pool of ideas. It involves listing the existing attribute(s) of each dimension of the problem and providing as many alternatives as possible (including wild and off-beat ones) for each attribute. Combinations of the alternatives generated can lead to new ideas and creative insights. Undoubtedly, the more remote/wilder the alternatives, the more novel/unique are the outcomes. While some outcomes may be impractical, other practical ones that may have earlier been overlooked have an opportunity to emerge (Khandwalla 2004). Moreover, unusual/impractical combinations can be considered as they can throw up further ideas that are worth pursuing (Proctor 1999). Morphological analysis can be used to generate ideas for products and processes and it works best when the problem under consideration has two or three dimensions (Proctor 1999).

For example: Create new socialization/induction programs for organizations, using morphological analysis.

Dimensions	Existing attributes	Alternative ideas
Venue	Hotels, banquet halls, office premises	Building top, underwater, inside pool, in air, forest, mountain top, island, beach, hospital, circus, zoo, pool side
Dress code	Formal, business casuals, casuals	Swim suit, party wear, newspapers, leaves, fancy dress, Halloween dresses (scary ones), all woolens, ghost wear
Activities	Formal sessions	Games, dances, songs, prayers, excursions
Food	Western/Continental, Indian, Chinese, vegetarian, non-vegetarian	Mediterranean, no food, pot-luck, health food, diet food, vegetarian for non-vegetarians, non-vegetarian for vegetarians
Time of the day	Office time	Early morning, late evening, whole night
Invitees	Company employees, managers	Families, clients, customers

The ideas that emerge from the alternatives suggested for each feature provide possible solutions/leads for possible solutions. It is possible that one may combine the ideas from several alternatives in the search for solutions.

Your task

Plan an innovative recruitment interview, using the morphological analysis process (10 minutes).

COMPONENTIAL DETAILING

Instructor guidelines

Objectives

To appreciate the contribution of componential detailing as an ideating mechanism.

Time

Three hours.

Material

(1) Art material including chart paper, glaze paper, crepe paper, paints, paint brushes, palettes, felt pens, crayons and color pencils.

(2) Stationery items including pencils, erasers, sharpeners, gum, scissors and cellotape.

(3) Magazines for pictures (magazines covering a variety of topics such as business, cookery, travel, fashion, and so on, should be included to provide a range of pictures).

(4) Classrooms (one for each group) equipped with CD playing facilities.

(5) Componential detailing worksheet (the number of copies must match the number of participants).

(6) Module 3 reflections sheet (the number of copies must match the number of participants).

(7) Take-home assignment 3 (the number of copies must match the number of participants).

(8) Module 3 reading handout (the number of copies must match the number of participants).

Procedure

(1) Introduce participants to the concept of componential detailing, relying on an example if required, and linking it to relayering.

(2) Divide the class into groups of six each.

(3) Distribute the "Componential detailing" worksheet to the participants in such a manner that some groups complete task 1, and others, task 2.

(4) Assign each group to a separate classroom and let them commence the work. They may take 120 minutes to complete the task.

(5) Each group may then be called upon to present their work. The presentation should describe the process/experience of componential detailing followed by the group (including a display of the pictures) as well as the outcomes/solutions developed by the group for the assigned task. Instructor may provide feedback on process and outcome.

(6) Wrap up the workshop by going over relayering and its techniques.

(7) Participants are asked to fill out Module 3 reflections sheet.

(8) Module 3 reading handout and take-home assignment 3 may now be distributed.

A suggested problem is provided in the following pages. Instructors may select problems of contemporary relevance for this activity. Depending on the problem selected, instructors may wish to assign participants particular tasks, as has been done in the above stated problem.

COMPONENTIAL DETAILING

Worksheet

Suggested by Wakin (cited in Proctor 1999), componential detailing is a group relayering associational technique that involves the following procedures:

(1) The group as a whole analyzes the problem at hand to identify its different components.

(2) The features of each component are then listed.

(3) The group divides into sub-groups and different problem components are allocated to different sub-groups for further work.

(4) Each sub-group develops a picture of their component, including as many details as possible (This could be a drawing/painting/sculpture/collage, and so on or a combination of these). This picture indicates how the sub-group views the component and could represent their conceptualization of the problem/wild ideas that come to their mind. Sub-group members can develop their pictures either collectively as a single unit/each individual member can develop a separate picture of his or her own/sub-group members could work on the same canvas but with each one using different corners of it and working individually on their own corner/sub-group members can work simultaneously collectively and individually so that they work on the same picture by individually and randomly adding on their ideas to other members' contributions (so one person's ideas become the stimuli for another person's ideas but there is no need for logic/rationality to guide the process of adding on).

(5) The pictures developed by all the sub-groups are collected and displayed together as a single collage, in an order decided by the group.

(6) The group, as a whole, reviews the collage for ideas which serve as stimuli for solutions rather than solutions in themselves. These ideas, which are derived from the collage as a whole or from parts of it, could be used as they are or they could be joined together or they could be further developed. They could inspire even more ideas. Ideas may start out as wild and unfeasible, and hence they may have to undergo several refinements before they are amenable to application.

Your task

Task 1

Read the case of Candyze, and then use componential detailing as outlined above to complete the following task:

You are a group of school students. Take a stand on the issue and develop an elaborate plan to back-up/operationalize your stand.

Task 2

Read the case of Candyze, and then use componential detailing as outlined above to complete the following task:

You are Magnify. Develop a comprehensive strategy to counter an attack from Candyze and to garner sustained public opinion in your favor from all sections of society.

Each group will occupy a single classroom. You may use any of the materials provided as part of the course in the completion of the activity. While you must work in your group guided by the principles of componential detailing, you may disperse from the group to get additional material/information/inspiration, and so on, should this be in keeping with group norms.

Candyze

Candyze, a leading brand of confectionery in the city, manufactures lozenges, jujubes, toffees, chocolates, lollipops, éclairs and mints in a variety of flavors, colors and shapes. Children of all ages are loyal customers, and all schools, whether public or private, in the city stock the whole range of Candyze's sweets.

Candyze's products and reputation came under the scanner about six months ago when mildew was observed on its jujubes. Taking the issue seriously, the city administration banned the sale of Candyze's products in schools, simultaneously ordering a probe into the matter. Candyze's management claims that the issue is a political one—the city administration is using it as a means to build up goodwill with the citizens and to spruce up its image. Industry observers maintain that such a ban achieves very little as children can purchase Candyze's confectionery in retail stores outside the premises of their schools.

Magnify, a consumer rights protection agency, has begun to investigate the matter independently. They are conducting inquiries on all Candyze's products to study various dimensions relating to the quality of the offerings. Candyze's management has responded to Magnify's move by initiating its own study. It claims that the researchers it has engaged are scientists of international repute who will establish the quality of its products. Candyze's management has also launched a campaign questioning Magnify's credibility. They allege that Magnify lacks the accreditation to conduct the tests required to certify food quality.

Notwithstanding the differing viewpoints, the city administration's ban on Candyze's products has made some dent on the company's sales figures, which have dropped by about 20 per cent.

Component–feature listing table

Component \ Feature					

MODULE 3 REFLECTIONS SHEET

Take a few minutes to recollect and note down your thoughts, feelings and actions on completion of today's workshop. While the questions below will give you some leads, they are not meant to be exhaustive.

About today's workshop

(1) Was this problem solving different to what I usually do? If yes, in what way?

(2) Was this different to the exercises I did last week? If yes, how and why? How do I feel about adopting such a problem solving style?

(3) How did I perform? Were there any factors like thoughts and feelings influencing me during the problem solving process— and how did they contribute to my task completion? What resources/supports (including intrapersonal ones) did I rely on during today's exercises? Was I conscious of what I was doing/ thinking/feeling during this time?

(4) What changes do I see in myself? Anything that I need to work on?

(5) How did I feel about working in a group as compared to working individually—what are my preferences and under what circumstances? What were the facilitating/constraining factors?

About myself

(1) How have my cognitive processes and sense of self changed over the last three weeks?

(2) Do I apply creative thinking techniques easily, without effort and consciousness, or do I have to remind myself to think creatively?

(3) Do I see value/benefit in the use of creative thinking?

(4) Which areas require further strengthening?

(5) In way does Workshop 3 take this process forward?

(6) Are there any areas that I need to work on/improve? If so, how do I plan to do so?

TAKE-HOME ASSIGNMENT 3

This assignment must be completed and submitted by the next workshop. You may use extra sheets as required.

(1) As part of your ecological sensitivity:

How many different fruits have you eaten in your life?

....

....

....

What are the different kinds of furniture in your office/institute?

....

....

....

(2) What are the most unusual uses you can think of for the following objects? List as many as you can, keeping in mind the principles of originality, fluency and flexibility.

Stapler

....

....

....

Eraser

....

....

....

Postal stamp

....

....

....

(3) What responses strike you immediately when you are faced with the following stimulus? Try to keep your response as remote/unusual/uncommon as possible.

An immediate deadline

....

....

....

An unco-operative team

....

....

....

(4) What idea emerges in your mind when you think of a concrete object and a sensory experience simultaneously, as in the following instances?

A whiteboard and melodious sounds

....

....

....

An apple and rapid heartbeats

....

....

....

(5) Combine the following antitheses to come up with an original idea:

Perseverance and laziness

....

....

....

Familiar and strange

....

....

....

Night and Day

. . . .
. . . .
. . . .

(6) Use the concept of elaboration to develop the following object/ idea into a creative/original/innovative final product.

Punch

. . . .
. . . .
. . . .

Gum

. . . .
. . . .
. . . .

(7) How would you use a question bank to increase gender sensitivity at the workplace?

. . . .
. . . .
. . . .

(8) How would you use a question bank to create economic safety nets for Indian society?

. . . .
. . . .
. . . .

(9) How would you use morphological analysis to create completely new and original Organizational Development (OD) programs?

. . . .
. . . .
. . . .

(10) Use morphological analysis to help Jason and Jennifer come up with good ideas to develop Angel's Footprint.

Angel's Footprint

Terekhol, a little known fort village of Goa, remains off the beaten track from mainstream tourists. It's coastline combines sandy beaches and steep cliffs, both kissed by the sea. Terekhol retains its pristine, virgin beauty, providing tourists an opportunity to fuse with nature. It's limited engagement with technology allows for regression to a rustic way and pace of life.

Capitalizing on this celestial setting are Jason and Jennifer who run Angel's Footprint, a medium-sized, no frills, boarding and lodging facility at Terekhol. The USP of Angel's Footprint is the tranquility and peace it offers, derived essentially from its integration with nature and a natural way of life. It is the perfect spot to reconnect with oneself and with the universe.

The 20 rooms of Angel's Footprint are furnished with minimal cane furniture, and lights and fans comprise the only electric fittings. Traditional Goan fare is served at a common self-service dining room. The facility has numerous outdoor and indoor spaces to hang around, some of which allow for complete solitude. A recreation cupboard houses books and music CDs as well as basic sports/games equipment for activities such as badminton, throwball, scrabble, ludo, playing cards, and so on. Jason, Jennifer and their staff of 10 people oversee the entire facility, providing courteous and efficient service.

The publicity of Angel's Footprint has been exclusively by word of mouth and the character and quality of its offering has ensured an evergrowing list of faithful clientele.

This ideal state of affairs is set to change. In a bid to ensure that Goa's tourism potential is totally capitalized upon, the Ministry of Tourism has, among other things, identified promising locations that have so far received scant attention. Terekhol is one of these.

Promoting Terekhol as "Paradise on Earth," the ministry has invited major players from India's hotel and holiday resort industries to develop the place, and many of them have responded with interest. Jason and Jennifer have grown extremely worried as a result of the turn of events. They are preoccupied as to how to ensure that Angel's Footprint survives while retaining its current uniqueness.

(11) Read the following case and identify the problem(s) to work on. Once the problem(s) has/have been identified, then solve it/them using combinations of attributes that emerged from the force fitting trigger cards shown to you during Workshop 3. Combinations should be so drawn up that each combination comprises three attributes, one from each trigger card. This combination should serve as a stimulation for ideation, operating as the starting point in the search for solutions.

Celeste Solutions

Shruti was the Vice President (VP), Marketing, at Celeste Solutions. She had moved to this job after a five year stint as Assistant Vice President (AVP), Marketing, with a Fast Moving Consumer Goods (FMCG) firm. Shruti had been a gold medallist throughout her academic career, and in her professional life, she had displayed sharp analytical skills, possessed up-to-date marketing knowledge and was known to be an excellent communicator. Shruti's move from FMCG to Information Technology (IT) was part of her career plan to be involved with global technological developments, and at the outset, she was confident that she possessed the skills and experience to demonstrate outstanding performance in her new role. Two months into her job at Celeste, Shruti was no longer sure that her expectations would be fulfilled.

It seemed to Shruti that she and Arvind, the Chief Executive Officer (CEO) of Celeste, could not see eye-to-eye on anything. There was considerable divergence in their understanding of the market. Arvind was clear that the market was about to saturate and that Celeste would be in a vulnerable position if it did not guard its position carefully. An aggressive marketing outlook was inevitable, he felt. Shruti was firm in her view that the market was still to mature, and hence chose softer marketing strategies. This difference in viewpoints, which emerged during the initial phases of interaction, translated into an ever-present impasse between Arvind and Shruti. Yet Shruti was unsure as to how to handle the situation—Arvind was after all her boss and she could not openly defy or disagree with him. Moreover, her job at Celeste was a step ahead in terms of designation and a move into the sector of her choice—quitting would mean giving up things that were important to her and would hurt her career. Shruti decided to wait and watch for sometime before doing anything—perhaps Arvind would realize her capability over time and things would settle down. But Shruti's hopes were short-lived.

A run-in between Arvind and Shruti took place once again that morning, leaving Shruti deeply perturbed. Shruti had prepared a press release announcing Celeste's imminent product launch. At the end of the morning corporate strategy meeting, Arvind asked Shruti about the press release. Shruti's reply did not quite convince Arvind of the approach she was taking and he wanted to see the draft.

Shruti brought it over to his office. The headline read: "Celeste launches new software." Arvind's immediate reaction was one of irritation but he held back from expressing it. Instead, he patiently pointed out to Shruti that her press release, especially the headline, lacked the attention-grabbing quality it called for. Given its tone, the item would be completely overlooked by readers. Arvind knew that this would not do. Celeste was surrounded by fierce competition and needed every bit of publicity that it could possibly get in order to maintain its position in the market. And ultimately, its ability to survive would reflect Arvind's leadership capability.

Arvind suggested that Shruti use a headline that read "Celeste's new software set to revolutionize the corporate world." While Shruti insisted that an understated headline was more appropriate for the kind of news they wished to share, Arvind responded, "It is important for the press release to highlight the new product and to demonstrate confidence and strength. The media tend to discount press releases and an understatement will get completely ignored. They will feel that we have nothing to say and will just put it aside."

Shruti pursed her lips and went back to her office. She mulled over her interactions with Arvind. Nothing she did seemed to be good enough for him. But more than that, what irked her was his assumption that he knew more about her field of work than she herself did. Shruti recalled her performance in her earlier organization—her decisions had always been on target and her judgment had always been astute. As a result, the top management had always sought her perspective prior to making strategic decisions. But at Celeste, Shruti felt that her work was always being questioned. Shruti believed that this stemmed from Arvind's engineering background, which, in her view, did not provide him with a sufficient understanding of marketing imperatives, thereby leading him to doubt her work. Shruti was inundated with misgivings and was completely non-plussed as to what to do.

Arvind, on the other hand, had his own story to relate. To begin with, Arvind had harbored numerous reservations about Shruti's appointment at her current designation. In his view, though her earlier performance was flawless, since it was not contextualized in the IT sector, she needed some time to understand and work within the complexities of this sector, and hence an appointment at AVP level would have been more appropriate. Arvind had found himself unsupported by Celeste's Chairperson on this point—the latter's point was that Shruti's academic and professional performances, apart from being outstanding, demonstrated both her ability to handle complexity and her cognitive flexibility to relate to different contexts. Shruti's appointment as VP, Marketing, at Celeste was thus decided by the Chairperson. Yet following her joining Celeste, Arvind had observed a couple of occasions when Shruti's decisions and judgments were incorrect.

Though Arvind put it down to Shruti's lack of familiarity with the IT sector, he believed that it was necessary to discuss the errors with her in order to guide her and ensure that they were not repeated. He believed that providing her with a comprehensive idea of the IT sector was imperative. But discussing matters with her proved to be disastrous. Shruti turned completely defensive and rigidly insisted on her points, citing her past performance as evidence and tangentially referring to Arvind's engineering background as a limitation of his understanding of her work. The meeting ended in a deadlock, with distrust and dislike on both sides. Arvind believed that his concern stemmed from the volatile and competitive nature of Celeste's market environment. The slightest error could precipitate irreversible damage which both Celeste and Arvind could ill afford. At the same time, Arvind was fully aware that since Shruti was the Chairperson's choice, he had to tread carefully. "How should I move forward?," he asked himself.

(12) Read the case and answer the questions that follow:

Eve's

In the course of her work as an independent commercial artist based in Mumbai, Seema interacted with many corporate personnel. As she observed the increasing number of women joining the corporate sector, Seema also realized the paucity of choice these women faced in terms of acquiring appropriate office wear. Seema felt convinced that there were good business opportunities available, not just because the territory was virtually untouched but also because economic liberalization was creating a large job market for women. After deliberating the matter over in her mind for some months, Seema decided to foray into the field with her own line of clothing.

Financing the venture with her own savings and with a loan, Seema began Eve's, a fashion label that served the metro's growing number of highly paid career women. Seema set up an outlet in the heart of South Mumbai's business locality, offering professional women colorful and comfortable clothes that were contemporary but elegant, catering to different seasons and in Indian and Western styles, allowing customers a wide range to choose from. Being able to cater to a group whose requirements were largely ignored so far, Eve's experienced immediate and resounding success. Seema was emboldened to set up three more outlets, one each located in Central Mumbai, the Western suburbs and Navi Mumbai.

All Eve's outlets were staffed by women only. Women were selected on the basis of their communication skills, emotional sensing and displaying abilities, understanding of working women's issues, customer sensitivity and fluency in English. They underwent rigorous training which oriented them to Eve's organizational culture and to the customer interaction skills expected of them. Following an evaluation of their learning at this stage, the trainees moved to the outlet floor where they observed seniors interacting with customers. Next, they were permitted to interact with customers under the supervision of their seniors. Successful completion of this phase allowed them to operate independently on the outlet floor.

Eve's success stemmed not just from the fact that it was fulfilling a void in the women's clothing space but also (and critically so) from the strong connectedness it maintained with consumers. The selection and training of outlet staff made a critical difference to the quality of customer interaction—customers reported feeling very comfortable at Eve's. The store personnel seemed to understand their needs completely and responded with interest and respect. Moreover, Eve's also staffed "interfacers" whose role was to spend time talking to customers to understand their needs and preferences. The information was ploughed back into the planning, design and production departments, with the result that the product range showed almost complete convergence with customer requirements.

Eve's expansion plans included not just other metros but Tier 2 cities as well. Seema's business contacts in Tier 2 cities informed her of the desire of many small stand-alone retail clothing outlets in these cities to sell off their businesses as these were no longer viable in the face of stiff competition from burgeoning retail chain groups. Seema and her strategy team considered buying out these businesses and using them as a launching pad for Eve's to be a good proposition. Turning her attention to Pune and Nagpur, both Tier 2 cities in the same state as Mumbai, Seema took over two retail outlets each in Pune and in Nagpur. The takeover terms and conditions included absorbing all the personnel working with the original store into Eve's. And this was where Eve's problems started.

The stores that Eve's took over employed mainly male attendants whose proficiency in English was either poor or non-existent. Moreover, there was huge variation within the service and customer orientation of the employees within and across these stores, in addition to a variation between the culture of Eve's and that of these stores. Seema and her team, recognizing the need for socializing their new employees, designed a comprehensive and intensive acculturation program. Apart from this program, training in customer interaction skills and English was given. The training in English was to continue over the long term so that fluency could be achieved.

After their participation in the program, the new employees returned to the outlet floor where they were joined by staff from Eve's Mumbai outlets. English language training continued simultaneously. Yet neither the training nor the presence of experienced personnel seemed to make a difference to the performance of the new employees. They continued with their earlier style of working which was quite different to that of Eve's. The customer connectedness that Eve's was so proud of was completely compromised. The effect was felt, not just in terms of the number of customers who visited the store and in terms of sales performance—the real casualty was the reputation and brand perception of Eve's. The chain was seen as harboring two sets of standards—one for larger cities and one for smaller cities, with stores in larger cities providing better quality service compared to those in the smaller cities. This was interpreted by people living in the smaller cities to mean that Eve's did not actually value them.

Seema was unclear as to how to go forward, given that she had already invested huge resources in the takeover and the remodeling of the new stores and given that she had agreed to absorb all the personnel. She also had ambitious takeover plans for other tier cities and expansion plans for other metros. In the meanwhile, her competitors were forging ahead.

(*a*) Identify the issues of the case, using your learning of changing mindsets/schema as a basis.

(*b*) Use the following random stimulus to generate alternatives to solve the problem, moving from wild, remote ideas to innovative, practical and elaborate solutions.

City traffic

(This poem has been written by Professor Ernesto Noronha, Indian Institute of Management, Ahmedabad)

> It's a jungle where silence makes you feel easy
> You feel eerie when it is noisy
> There are several beasts—black, blue and red—
> Whose presence makes you feel the dread
> They have no system of control
> White hats are helpless, can't stop 'em roll.

They just can't wait, they want to run,
They are never disqualified by the gun.
Thus there are clashes every day,
For criss-crossing each other's ways.
The big wild cats are usually fierce,
Sometimes they screech into the ears.
Seldom do they give way,
And want others to do what they say.
Threateningly they come to pounce,
The little ones soon renounce

While the smaller ones have their own play,
They many a times try a zigzag way.
They don't believe in sticking to lanes
As if to say, time is to be gained.
They sometimes meet their match,
And try to make one another catch
They pressurize the White Hat, to let them pass,
By slowly inching on the cross.
They always seem to feel
Like zoo animals set free.

There are others who laze around,
They park themselves on any ground
They seem to laugh as others squeeze,
And breathe in the polluted breeze.
There is no hope that the jungle will improve,
Lack of self-restraint is the proof.

(13) List out all the processes in your organization. Select one and
work on 20 innovative changes to improve it.

. . . .
. . . .
. . . .

(14) List out all the offerings of your organization. Select one and
work on 20 innovative changes to improve it.

. . . .
. . . .
. . . .

(15) Come up with 20 different ways in which presentations can be made such that their effectiveness is enhanced.

....
....
....

(16) Are there any areas in which your organization/institute needs to be creative?

....
....
....

(17) Think back to any night dream that you have had which stands out vividly in your memory. Write it down in detail. Analyze it for its ideational quality, keeping in mind the principles of fluency, flexibility and originality. Then examine it from the point of view of its utility. If it had to be lived out in real life, how would the principle of elaboration apply?

....
....
....

(18) Think of the most challenging role/task that you handle in your student/professional life. What innovations can you come up with to make this role/task easier?

....
....
....

Module 4

Fantasy Trails

INTRODUCTORY NOTE

Fantasy trails are derived from the creativity technique of synectics. Developed by William Gordon and George Prince, synectics is a group creativity technique that engages two mental processes to promote the occurrence of creative breakthroughs (Proctor 1999). Making the strange familiar involves fitting the unfamiliar entity into an acceptable pattern to make room for the strangeness. The mind compares the given strangeness with data previously known, and in terms of these data, converts the strangeness into familiarity. The basic procedures involved are analysis, generalization and analogy. Analysis is the process of breaking down a complexity into its component parts. Generalization is the intellectual act of identifying patterns among the component parts. Analogy is the equivalent of asking oneself, "What in my knowledge or experience is like this?" (Prince 1968). Making the familiar strange entails a conscious attempt to achieve a new look at the same old world, people, ideas, feelings, and things, by distorting, or transposing the everyday ways of looking and responding. This allows for a problem to be viewed from different perspectives, stimulating ideation based upon these various perspectives (Gordon 1961).

Below are the steps involved in a synectics exercise as described by Prince (1968).

(1) **Problem as given (PAG):** Once the group assembles, group members are apprised of the problem as defined by those seeking a solution to it.

(2) **Analysis:** An expert familiar with the problem explains it to the group, making the strange problem familiar to group members.

(3) **Purge:** Group members put forward all the solutions that immediately come to their minds and these are kept aside. Identification of the familiar paves the way for making the familiar strange, setting the stage for the exploration of unusual alternatives.

(4) **Problem as understood (PAU):** Each group member must now restate the problem such that different perspectives, including those embodying the subjectivity of the particular group member as well as those that are wild and remote, emerge. Using this list, the group may finalize several PAUs which provide diverse approaches to the problem.

(5) **Evocative question (EQ):** In order to stimulate associational thinking in the attempt to generate unique alternatives and creative solutions to the problem, three categories of evocative questions that result in three kinds of analogical or metaphorical answers are posed.

(a) Direct analogies involve the actual comparison of parallel facts, knowledge or technology, requiring a search of one's experience and knowledge for some phenomenon that is alike or has some similar relationship with the problem at hand.

(b) Personal analogies call for playing the role of entities either human and/or non-human that figure in the problem. By role playing how that entity feels and acts, one gets insights into the problem.

(c) Symbolic analogies are created by selecting a key word from the problem and by expressing its essential subjective meaning through a highly compressed, poetic phrase. For instance, the symbolic analogy for the keyword "commitment" could be "contrived genuineness". Similarly, the symbolic analogy for the keyword "conflict" could be "engaging deliberations". The analogy is then used as a stimulus to generate ideas and alternatives.

(6) **Examination:** The group selects an analogy and examines it to produce descriptive facts and superfacts/speculative and strange facts.

(7) **Force fit (FF):** Analogical mechanisms, with their facts and superfacts, do not directly provide solutions to the problem but must be force-fitted to the problem. Force fits provide the raw

materials for new lines of speculation, resulting in refocusing the problem so that it may be seen in a new way as well as in triggering ideas and alternatives that serve as potential solutions.

(8) **Viewpoint:** Appropriately developed analogical mechanisms give rise to multiple potential solutions, also known as viewpoints.

(9) **Excursion:** Excursion refers to the synectics procedure from the PAU stage to the force fit stage. If no new viewpoint is developed, another excursion is undertaken through all or part of the procedure. That is, sometimes new analogies can be developed to the same EQ or a new EQ may be used, or when a force fit attempt reveals a new aspect to the problem, a new PAU may be stated (Prince 1968).

Hicks (1991) suggests the use of a fantasy or imaging excursion which often works dramatically well and produces the most innovative ideas. For a fantasy or imaging excursion, the group is asked to describe a mental picture/story inspired by the last item in a word association preliminary exercise. One person will lead off and then every other person in the group has to add to the story. They should be invited to jump in whenever they like, having been instructed that the more colorful, outlandish, weird and exotic the story, the better. If the story tends to stagnate on some minute detail of one particular image, the leader can ask someone to make something surprising happen. Conversely, if images are insufficiently developed because storytellers move too quickly to other images, the leader can pin people to one scenario by asking for more detail. People may be anxious about producing mental images in public and about their ability to contribute to the story. It is, however, the violent changing of directions and having to build another mental image after the destruction of the first that makes the story rich in speculation and evocative images. When every group member has had at least one chance to contribute to the story, the leader stops the imaging and asks the group to replay the story in their minds so that it stimulates ideas for potential solutions to the problem (Proctor 1999).

While a synectics session works best in a diverse group of six to eight people (Khandwalla 2004), the role of the leader is critical. Synectics group sessions are always conducted by a leader who is primarily responsible for keeping the problem investigation within the confines of the synectics process and for ensuring the most efficient generation, development and use of analogical material. The leader is neither a judge (passing on the merits of a contribution) nor a moderator (comparing disparate contributions) nor a chairperson (who prepares an agenda and keeps out extraneous contributions) (Prince 1968).

ACTIVITY SEQUENCE

(1) Reveries
(2) Winning Dyads
(3) Weaving Stories
(4) Distilling Stories

REVERIES

Instructor guidelines

Objectives

To help participants realize that daydreams are natural ideating mechanisms, serving as gateways to our imagination and highlighting our capacity to be creative. Daydreams could serve as the genesis of important ideas and associations, setting the stage for great breakthroughs.

Time

Sixty minutes.

Material

Light instrumental music to create an appropriate atmosphere prior to initiating daydreaming.

Procedure

(1) At the outset, the instructor should ensure the presence of a calm and peaceful atmosphere that sets the tone for the exercise.

(2) Ask participants to close their eyes, relax their bodies, and unleash their imagination for a while. Elaborate that their imagination should wander freely, without inhibition or censorship, for a few minutes, following its own path, and that they should absorb and be absorbed by the experience.

(3) After five or ten minutes, ask participants to open their eyes. Participants may be asked to share their daydreams. Following this, participants may be asked to share their experience of engaging in the act of daydreaming.

(4) A discussion may be held on the value of daydreaming in terms of providing ideas that could contribute to one's life in various ways or in terms of bringing to the fore one's capacity to create stories. The activity may be concluded by highlighting ways of capitalizing on and capturing daydreams.

WINNING DYADS

Instructor guidelines

Objectives

This activity aims at helping participants revise the concepts they have learnt so far via an opportunity to express themselves creatively.

Time

Sixty minutes.

Material

(1) Large plastic/cardboard container with slips of colored paper containing the various concepts (a possible list is given at the end of this activity) that have been covered so far in the course (There should be an even number of slips).

(2) Plastic/cardboard container with slips containing names of one half of the participants (Group A).

(3) Plastic/cardboard container with slips containing names of the other half of the participants (Group B).

(4) Art material including chart paper, glaze paper, crepe paper, paints, paint brushes, palettes, felt pens, crayons and color pencils.

(5) Stationery items including pencils, erasers, sharpeners, gum, scissors and cellotape.

(6) Blackboard with chalk/whiteboard with markers.

(7) Prize for the winning group.

Procedure

(1) Divide the participants into two groups, namely Group A and Group B, each having equal numbers.

(2) Pick out one slip with a participant name from container A and one from container B.

(3) Ask these participants to come to the front of the class.

(4) The participant from Group A must pick up a slip from the concept box and must proceed to creatively but non-verbally provide a clue to the participant from Group B so that the latter may guess the concept. The participant from Group A is given one chance to provide the clue and the participant from Group B is given one chance to guess the concept.

(5) If the participant from Group B guesses the concept correctly, both Group A and Group B are awarded one point each. The participant from Group B then has to explain the concept to the class, and if he/she does so correctly, then Group B is awarded one point.

(6) If the participant from group B is unable to guess the concept based on participant A's clueing, neither Group A nor Group B gets any point. However, the participant from Group A has to explain the concept to the class—if he/she can do so correctly, he/she gets one point; if he/she cannot do so, one negative point is awarded to Group A.

(7) The next round then begins, proceeding in the manner described above—however, this time, the participant from Group B picks up a slip of paper from the concept box and provides the clue to the participant picked from Group A.

(8) The winning group may be given a prize.

LIST OF CONCEPTS FOR WINNING DYADS

(1) Convergent thinking
(2) Question bank
(3) Reversal
(4) Homospatial process
(5) Flexibility
(6) Random stimulation
(7) Change of entry point
(8) Creative outcome
(9) Sublime creativity
(10) Force fitting triggers
(11) Restructuring
(12) Componential detailing
(13) Imagination
(14) Incubation
(15) Elaboration
(16) Bisociation

The above list is illustrative and the instructor may use concepts of his/her choice.

WEAVING STORIES

Instructor guidelines

Objectives

To experience the use of stories as an ideating mechanism in problem solving. Weaving stories involves creating the story while distilling stories entails using ideas and associations from the stories to solve problems.

Time

Sixty minutes.

Material

(1) Audio-cassette recorders (one for each group).

(2) Blank audio-cassettes (one for each group).

(3) Power source to operate the audio-cassette recorders (either batteries or electrical connections).

(4) Picture and word force fitting trigger cards.

(5) Classrooms (one for each group).

(6) Weaving stories worksheet (the number of copies must match the number of participants).

Procedure

(1) Explain the fantasy trail process and distribute the "Weaving stories" worksheet.

(2) Divide the participants into groups of six each and assign each group to a separate classroom.

(3) Provide each group with an audio-cassette recorder, a blank audio-cassette and a power source.

(4) Place the picture and word trigger cards on the instructor's table so that participants may use these as initiating stimuli, if they so wish.

(5) Participants are given 20–30 minutes to create and record their stories, followed by another 20–30 minutes to listen to them and note down the ideas/associations that strike them.

WEAVING STORIES

Worksheet

The fantasy trail technique is a group technique, inspired by William Gordon's (1961) and George Prince's (1968) synectics. In this technique, the group creates a fantastic/weird story that is then relied upon to provide associations and ideas to solve problems. The following example illustrates how this can be done.

Step 1: The group/group member selects a key word/a phrase/ stimulus (this could be a picture or an object).

Eg: A picture of snow-capped mountains.

Step 2: The group sits in a circle and weaves a story using this stimulus as the opening sentence. In creating the story, each group member contributes a sentence in turn which need not be linked to the preceding sentence. Group members should allow their mind to freewheel, being completely generative when weaving the story—they should go on a "fantasy excursion", adding to the story any outlandish, weird or exotic ideas that come to their mind, regardless of the sequencing of thoughts/events, and so on. This step lasts for about 20–30 minutes and the story must be audio-recorded.

Following is the example of a story woven by a group of six people (P1, P2, P3, P4, P5 and P6), using the picture of a barbeque party as a stimulus:

P1 - Flying, he reached a snow-capped mountain.

P4 - And started to talk and jump.

P5 - Then he reached Hogwarts.

P4 - In Hogwarts, he thought he would play Quidditch.

P3 - Then he hated flying brooms so he decided to use the aspirator...

P5 - Then he saw lizards which were all around.

P6 - So he thought it's time to change his form because he was God.

P3 - He thought to cook a cake.

P2 - And he decided to celebrate his birthday.

P1 - The cake had three tiers covered in cream.

P4 - And there was a photo of him on each edge.

P5 - He only wanted the cherry on the cake.

P6 - So he ate the cherry not knowing it was the forbidden cherry.

P2 - So, he no more was God.

P1 - Now he is mortal man who must eat whole cake.

P5 - So he ate the whole cake.

P4 - And it went down his digestive tract in places unknown and which should not be known. Then one day it all came out.

P2 - And so the commode was discovered.

P4 - And now the cake was on its way to the ocean.

P5 - Through the same system which existed in the rivers.

P6 - So once it got to the ocean it was eaten by a big fish.

P3 - The fish went ill.

P2 - And fish thought she should see a doctor.

P1 - There were a lot of things in the fish's belly—big huge ships and some doctors also.

P4 - And there was a sea hospital in the form of a whale.

P5 - And the whale wanted to exhale.

P6 - I don't know from where?

P3 - She went to the North Pole because she was looking for the child she had lost.

P2 - The child was right there and she could identify him because of a mark on the chin.

P1 - Lost in the city cultural festival.

P4 - And she was surprised that her son was changed in five years.

P5 - In five years he had become a superstar.

P2 - And just in front of her, she dived into the center of the world.

P1 - There were lot of flowers in the center of the world.

P4 - And it was hot.

P5 - And there, water is boiling.

P6 - And where there is water and where there is lava, there are beaches. And it was really hot.

P3 - And he found there is some boiling water which was sweet.

P2 - And fish decided that it was too much to be in an ocean and she left for earth—land.

P3 - That's when the star exploded.

P2 - And the whole solar system was re-formed and there was a planet called Pluto.

P1 - Pluto was renamed Inspire.

P5 - And it was ruled by the dogs.

P6 - And just then there was a meteor explosion or meteor rain and it decided to surf on the meteor.

P3 - That was lot of fun.

P2 - She enjoyed it a lot but suddenly the meteor fell on the earth.

P1 - And there was a huge explosion and humans came out.

P4 - Once she had come back to earth, she decided to work in a volcano.

P5 - She worked for 10 years and then she retired.

P6 - And then there was one politician.

P3 - Worse than a meteor.

P2 - The worst crisis to hit human civilization.

Step 3: The group replays the story so that individual members can listen to it and allow ideas or associations (however remote or absurd) to emerge from it. These are noted down. Group members should not hesitate to note down their most weird thoughts.

Step 4: Group members, then, either individually or collectively, derive solutions from the absurd ideas/associations to solve the problem at hand. Initially, these solutions will be wild/unfeasible. The individual and/or group then refines the proposed solutions from remote to practical.

Your task

(1) Work in your group to create a story on the lines described above. Each group will occupy a single classroom, and will be provided with an audio-cassette recorder, a blank audio-cassette and a power source.

(2) You may use the picture and word trigger cards placed on the instructor's table as initiating stimuli, if your group so wishes.

(3) You have 20–30 minutes to create and record your stories, followed by another 20–30 minutes to listen to them and individually note down the ideas/associations that immediately strike you on hearing the story. Do not hesitate to write down your wildest/most remote idea/association.

DISTILLING STORIES

Instructor guidelines

Objectives

In continuation of weaving stories, this activity entails using ideas and associations from the stories to solve problems.

Time

Ninety minutes (this time would increase should the instructor decide to play some of the stories for the entire class to hear).

Material

(1) Weaving stories worksheet (these are now already with the participants, duly completed with ideas/associations from the stories they have just created in their groups).

(2) Distilling stories worksheet (the number of copies must match the number of participants).

(3) Module 4 reflections sheet (the number of copies must match the number of participants).

(4) Take-home assignment 4 (the number of copies must match the number of participants).

(5) Module 4 reading handout (the number of copies must match the number of participants).

Procedure

(1) Once the participants have identified ideas/associations from the stories that they have created, a problem may be given to them.

(2) Let them solve this problem individually.

(3) Participants may be given 60 minutes to complete this activity.

(4) Once participants reassemble, the stories of some groups may be played for everyone to listen to (additional time would have to be allocated for this).

(5) Following this, individual participants may be called upon to share their solutions to the problem and the instructor may provide feedback on the same.

(6) Wrap up the activity linking fantasy trails with synectics and with random stimulation.

(7) Participants may complete Module 4 reflections sheet. Module 4 reading handout and take-home assignment 4 may be distributed.

The problem that participants are expected to work on could be either a case or a contemporary business problem obtained from a business magazine.

DISTILLING STORIES

Worksheet

Read the case below and solve it using the ideas/associations you have just identified from the story, to help you find solutions. Your solutions may be weird and unfeasible initially, but you must refine them to make them realistic and elaborate.

Deal Home Retail

Deal Home Retail is an eight-year-old retail chain for groceries, FMCG and household products, with outlets in five Indian metros. Deal owns all its outlets and all the personnel working in these outlets are full-time employees of the organization.

Deal started out with 10 outlets and 200 people in a metro in western India. During these initial years, the management of Deal institutionalized a culture that emphasizes maturity, integrity, responsibility, self-directedness, egalitarianism and compassion. Deal's recruitment and selection processes ensured the perpetuation and reinforcement of these values, and as a result, Deal was staffed with self-driven and committed employees who put organizational interests above their own. Organizational control mechanisms were not required—on the contrary, the espousal of organizational values ensured organizational commitment and employee performance.

Deal's organizational structure was flat and promoted informal and open communication. Weekly open forum meetings across the hierarchy helped employees keep in touch with each other so that they understood each other's demands and pressures, and maintained supportive linkages with each other. Freedom and autonomy coexisted with trust and responsibility. Employees used the freedom given to them responsibly and this was illustrated via their decision-making and task performance. The positive intra-organizational atmosphere had a ripple effect on customer interaction. Being happy and satisfied at the workplace enabled employees to interact in a warm, sensitive and caring manner with customers. Thanks to the quality of customer interaction, customers provided Deal's employees with important feedback and insights that allowed them to enhance their service delivery and further improve customer satisfaction.

During its first five years, Deal's structure, culture and processes worked to its advantage, with the company reporting record profits and a record number of consumers each year.

It was during the process of expansion that Deal began to face numerous challenges. Deal's management decided to expand within the existing metro and to create a presence in four other metros too. This implied a five-fold increase in the number of outlets and employees. It was opined that this expansion would take place within Deal's current organizational framework.

Two years after the expansion plans were operationalized, Deal's top management began to notice a drop in performance. All financial indicators pointed to a decline. Considering the situation to be worrisome, the top management instituted a panel to establish the reasons behind this development.

The findings of the panel surprised Deal's top management. They found that the organizational dimensions that accounted for Deal's success during its early years were now working against it. The values of maturity, integrity, responsibility, self-directedness, egalitarian-ism and compassion—that helped Deal garner employee commitment and ensure organizational effectiveness—no longer operated as they had earlier. Instead of displaying behaviors that demonstrated these values, employees began to take advantage of the autonomy and trust they enjoyed. They frittered away their time, misused resources, made inappropriate decisions and disregarded customers. Though such behavior began with small groups of employees, it spread to other groups because of two reasons: first, the initial group of perpetrators went scot-free; and second, the committed hardworking group who found themselves fulfilling all work requirements reacted with resentment and adopted the recalcitrant group's behavior.

Deal's top management realized that allowing such behavior to continue would be detrimental for Deal's survival and progress, especially in the light of growing competition in the retail sector. At the same time, the top management group was not in favor of introducing stringent control mechanisms in the organization—they believed that such an approach would result in an atmosphere of mistrust and suspicion with adverse effects on intra-organizational communication, decision-making and support, and on customer service and satisfaction.

MODULE 4 REFLECTIONS SHEET

Take a few minutes to recollect and note down your thoughts, feelings and actions on completion of today's workshop. While the questions below will give you some leads, they are not meant to be exhaustive.

About today's workshop

(1) Was this problem solving different to what I usually do? If so, in what way?

(2) Was this different to the exercises I did last week? If so, how and why? How do I feel about adopting such a problem solving style?

(3) How did I perform? Were there any factors like thoughts and feelings influencing me during the problem solving process—and how did they contribute to my task completion? What resources/supports (including intrapersonal ones) did I rely on during today's exercises? Was I conscious of what I was doing/thinking/feeling during this time?

(4) What changes do I see in myself? Anything that I need to work on?

About myself

(1) How have my cognitive processes and sense of self changed over the last four weeks?

(2) Do I apply creative thinking techniques easily, without effort and consciousness, or do I have to remind myself to think creatively?

(3) Do I see value/benefit in the use of creative thinking?

(4) Which areas require further strengthening?

(5) In what way does Workshop 4 take this process forward?

(6) Are there any areas that I need to work on/improve? If so, how do I plan to do so?

TAKE-HOME ASSIGNMENT 4

This assignment must be completed and submitted by the next workshop. You may use extra sheets as required.

(1) Keeping in mind the relevance of changing mindsets, what are the different ways in which you can look at the following situations:

Social activists are hampering the process of development across the world.

....
....
....

Professionally managed organizations cannot compare with family-run businesses in matters of commitment.

....
....
....

(2) What are the most unusual uses you can think of for the following objects? List as many as you can, keeping in mind the principles of originality, fluency and flexibility.

Scissors

....
....
....

Paper clip

....
....
....

Phone

....
....
....

(3) What responses strike you immediately when you are faced
with the following stimulus? Try to keep your response as
remote/unusual/uncommon as possible.

An ethical decision

....
....
....

An unfair appraisal

....
....
....

(4) What idea emerges in your mind when you think of a concrete
object and a sensory experience simultaneously, as given in the
following instances?

A rocket and bitter taste

....
....
....

A memo and serrated surfaces

....
....
....

(5) Combine the following antitheses to come up with an original idea:

Integrity and dishonesty

....
....
....

Clear and hazy

....
....
....

Steam and ice

....
....
....

(6) Use the concept of elaboration to develop the following object/ idea into a creative/original/innovative final product.

Envelope

....
....
....

Pen drive

....
....
....

(7) Invent a new language.

....
....
....

(8) Find innovative ways of communicating via business/visiting cards.

. . . .

. . . .

. . . .

(9) In the previous take-home exercises, you listed out all the processes in your organization. Select another one and work on 20 innovative changes to improve it.

. . . .

. . . .

. . . .

(10) In the previous take-home exercises, you listed out all the offerings of your organization. Select another one and work on 20 innovative changes to improve it.

. . . .

. . . .

. . . .

(11) Come up with 20 different ways in which meetings can be held so that their effectiveness is enhanced.

. . . .

. . . .

. . . .

(12) Study the case below. Identify the problem using lateral thinking techniques for changing mindsets. Choose any random stimulus and use it to generate alternatives and develop solutions to the problem.

Eastworld metals

(This case has been developed jointly by the author and by Professor Ernesto Noronha, Indian Institute of Management, Ahmedabad).

Eastworld Metals, a private sector manufacturing firm located in an East Indian industrial town, came into existence in December 1922. The company produced tinplate through hot pack rolling and hot dip pinning. The company had six hot dip plants (HDPs) in 1951, to which it added one more plant in 1957, raising the capacity from 60,000 tonnes per annum to 70,000 tonnes per annum.

To keep pace with the technological developments, Eastworld Metals set up an electrolytic tinplating combination line in 1978, capable of producing electrolytic tinplate and tin free steel. The delay in commissioning the electrolytic tinplate plant (ETP), envisaged in the early 1970s, and its marginal utilization led to the first financial crisis that the company faced. In 1980, the company's losses were INR 60 million and its debt stood at INR 280.5 million. The company overcame the crisis only when the government eased the import duties on tin mill black plate (TMBP) between 1979–1983, and the financial institutions wrote off INR 30 million and converted INR 20 million to equity shares.

Nonetheless, the HDP continued to perform beyond its existing capacity. In 1985–86, the HDP produced at 118 per cent of its capacity and in 1987–88, it recorded a production of 84,757 tonnes which was 121 per cent of its capacity. By 1989, the mills had converted to sheet production. They produced electrical stampings, galvanized sheets (plain and corrugated), and black sheets for packaging. The manually operated rolling mills were also converted to semi-mechanized mills. The ETP, on the other hand, only functioned at 54 per cent of its capacity. The re-imposition of high import duty on TMBP continued to plague the ETP. This compelled the company to increase the selling price of tinplate considerably, resulting in many consumers shifting to other cheaper packaging media since the cost of imported tinplates was considerably cheaper than those indigenously produced.

To overcome these problems faced by the ETP, Eastworld Metals decided to set up a state-of-the-art cold rolling mill (CRM) in 1996. The capital expenditure on the cold rolling mill project was substantial, and therefore the company had a heavy debt servicing burden to pay in the coming years. Besides this, there was again a delay in its commissioning. The total capitalized cost for the CRM complex worked out to around INR 3090 million. The depreciation and interest charges on account of the delay of the commissioning of the cold-rolling mill project totaled INR 231.7 million in 1996–97. Eastworld Metals reported a loss of INR 270.2 million for 1996–97, against a profit of INR 43.3 million the previous year. By the end of 1996–97 fiscal year, the company had a term loan burden of INR 1779.5 million. The losses in 1997–98 went up to INR 610 million. The company notified the Board of Industrial and Financial Restructuring (BIFR) in the financial year 1998 of the erosion of its net worth by more than 50 per cent, with the accumulated losses of INR 751.4 million as on March 31, 1998. The HDP also began to suffer on account of shortage of raw material. Company A (a private manufacturing firm which was located in the same town, and which was a sister concern of Eastworld Metals), who supplied the raw material, had decided to stop its production of the same. Moreover, it was not possible to upgrade the plant any further. Further, financial institutions insisted on shutting down the 80-year-old HDP in favor of more advanced technologies.

To summarize, the HDP was a profit making unit whose functionality was curbed due to the lack of availability of raw material and due to obsolescence. The ETP, together with the CRM, was a modern unit, whose setting up had created huge debts for the company and was its main source of loss. Despite this difference between the two plants, the management of the company believed that saving ETP was a better long term option as it was a modernized plant that would help Eastworld Metals gain competitive advantage. HDP, on the other hand, being outdated and its raw material being unavailable, was selected for closure. It was believed that dismantling HDP would help to bail out ETP in the long run.

When the decision to close down the HDP was finalized, the management of Eastworld Metals decided to apply for its closure to the BIFR and to float a Voluntary Retirement Scheme (VRS) for the 2500 HDP workers who were facing imminent separation. The latter decision was made keeping in mind that should the closure be granted by the government, the compensation payable to the workers would be decided by the Industrial Disputes (ID) Act, 1947, and thus would be very meager, whereas a VRS program would provide better benefits and serve workers' interests more adequately. The management thus worked towards a VRS scheme. To do this, they checked the past records to see if there had been any such schemes in the past. A scheme from 1982 was found, and modified. Under the scheme, employees aged 50+ years were to receive 75 per cent of last drawn monthly salary payable per month upto 60 years while employees less than 50 years were to receive 75 per cent of last drawn monthly salary payable per month for 72 months (see Table II.1, Scheme 1). Additionally, medical benefits were to be provided (see Table II.1). Assistance and advice about investments was also to be given to workers during the process of separation. People from banks and other financial institutions like Industrial Development Bank of India (IDBI) and Unit Trust of India (UTI) were called to show the separating workers how best they could invest their money.

Table II.1 **Benefits under the Voluntary Retirement Scheme of Eastworld Metals**

---

1. **Under Scheme 1**
   Employees aged 50+ years: 75 per cent of last drawn monthly salary payable per month upto the age of 60 years.
   Employees less than 50 years: 75 per cent of last drawn monthly salary payable per month for 72 months.

2. **Under Scheme 2**
   Employees aged 50+ years: 100 per cent of last drawn monthly salary payable per month upto the age of 60 years.
   Employees aged less than 50 years: 100 per cent of last drawn monthly salary payable per month for 72 months.

3. **Medical benefits common to schemes 1 and 2**
   Medical benefits for self and dependents upto 60 years.

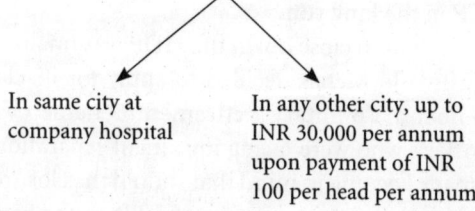

In same city at company hospital

In any other city, up to INR 30,000 per annum upon payment of INR 100 per head per annum

Medical benefits after 60 years—for self and spouse, as per rules for retiring employees.

When VRS was floated, about 700–800 workers came forward and availed of VRS under Scheme 1. However, the others resisted for two reasons: First, workers maintained that the closure order had not been granted by the government, and they also harbored doubts as to whether the government would permit closure since the HDP was a profit-making unit; and second, workers observed a lack of parity between the VRS schemes of their company and that of Company A (which was simultaneously downsizing via an extremely attractive VRS scheme). Workers expected a package similar to that being offered by Company A especially because both Eastworld Metals and Company A were sister concerns and the current Director, Personnel, of Eastworld Metals had earlier been working with Company A.

Workers questioned why they could not be absorbed in the ETP. Managers pointed out to them that they had been given an opportunity to do so some years ago when the ETP had begun its operation but they had not availed of it and there were no longer any vacancies there. Workers maintained that they had not transferred themselves from HDP to ETP at that time they had not believed that the HDP would actually close down since it was a profit-making unit.

The management of Eastworld Metals, being quite sure that the government would grant closure for the plant, realized that it was necessary to separate the workers and also to ensure that the separated workers took VRS. Therefore, with a view to attracting more workers, the benefits being provided under the VRS were enhanced. Under the revised scheme, employees aged 50+ years received 100 per cent of last drawn monthly salary payable per month upto the age of 60 years while employees less than 50 years old received 100 per cent of last drawn monthly salary payable per month for 72 months. Medical benefits continued as earlier (see Table II.1). Other modifications based on workers' aspirations were incorporated. The initial schemes gave a lumpsum payment. But workers indicated a preference for monthly payments as well as some concessions for housing, electricity and training for themselves and/or their children, so these were looked into and accommodated. Revisions in the scheme prompted another 700–800 workers to take VRS. However, more than 1,000 surplus men still remained on the rolls of the company, hoping that the government would not grant permission for closure.

Revisions in the compensation scheme, while fulfilling the object-ive of increasing the number of workers who opted for VRS, had un-foreseen negative repercussions. Workers who had taken VRS under the first scheme held agitations to mark their displeasure because of the inequity between the two schemes.

Implementing the VRS scheme was the task of the Human Resources (HR) department. But performing such a task presented the man-agers with numerous complex dilemmas. Interfacing management and workers was a tough balancing act. The management expected the HR managers to separate all the HDP workers, and this was tied in with their key result areas (KRAs). Weekly meetings between the HR managers and the management were held to review the former's progress and performance. HR managers were under tremendous pressure to deliver; their survival in the organization was at stake.

Yet facing the workers was not easy. The HR department had always enjoyed a good relationship with the workers and asking them to leave the organization put HR managers in a very difficult position. Indeed nothing in their training nor professional experience prepared the managers for this role, since they had been groomed to see their contribution as one of giving employment and developing people. Hence, rendering workers unemployed and presenting them with a bleak future created tremendous discomfort in the HR managers. HR managers expressed helplessness over their predicament: they had no choice except to ask workers to go if they had to fulfill management's expectations, and in the process, save the company and secure their own positions. Though they attempted as far as possible to maintain the interests of workers and preserve the goodwill they enjoyed with them, under pressure to perform and deliver, HR managers adopted force and pressure tactics with unrelenting workers.

Various alternatives were used. Those who refused to co-operate were threatened with transfers to lower level jobs, in order to humiliate them and force them to take VRS. While these threats worked in some cases, where they did not, they were translated into action. Another strategy was to threaten workers with dismissal.

The managers admitted that, in many instances, there was noth-ing voluntary about the VRS scheme: "There was nothing voluntary about it. Voluntary cases were rare. In 90 per cent of the cases, we forced them. But we never thought that we were doing anything wrong, because we had to save the company".

But workers, on their part, did not take anything lying down. They reacted with threats and abuses which became a way of life for the HR managers. One manager said: "There was bitterness and abuse, but no assault. I received some phone calls. Some were anonymous—they would abuse you and put it down. I also got calls from the police telling me not to pressurize workers, but I told them that the workers would have to go sooner or later".

Another stated: "They would gather in groups outside the gate and when I would pass in my car, they would make comments, 'He is management's *chamcha* (loyalist and informant).' They even followed my car once for some distance".

Some of the managers reported being attacked. Night soil was thrown into one officer's cabin and his car was stopped. Death threats were also received. In some cases, the managers' family members received threats.

Taking the threats seriously, the management of the company offered the HR managers security cover, transport, alternative accommodation for temporary periods, and was willing to even extend this support to their families, if the latter were receiving threats. But managers refused the security cover because there was a feeling that if they were seen with security, it would give the impression that they were afraid, and this would result in more threats.

Some HR managers had to go into hiding or leave the city temporarily to ensure their safety. They had to stay away from their homes for a while as cases were registered against them and warrants for their arrests had been issued. Movements of these managers were curtailed and police officials were kept informed about the developments.

An important consolation for the management and HR managers of Eastworld Metals was that they had ensured that all their actions were within the purview of the existing labor laws, and that in designing the VRS scheme, they had attempted to maximize the benefits for the separating workers.

(12) How would you use a question bank to minimize gossip and rumors at the workplace/institute?

....

....

....

(13) How would you use morphological analysis to promote your organization's corporate social responsibility (CSR) initiatives?

....
....
....

(14) Develop a business plan or strategy for your organization/ department/team/institute in any area of your choice.

....
....
....

(15) Take any product that you wish and create an advertisement campaign for it—your work should not only be innovative but also complete in all respects (including audio-visuals). It should also have a market value such that an advertising agency or the organization marketing the product will jump at the idea of using your advertisement.

....
....
....

Module 5

Essential Brainstorming

Commonly used as a generic term for creative thinking, brainstorming is believed to have been practiced in Asia over 3,000 years ago. A group creativity technique, brainstorming involves a cycle of expansion and contraction. Expansion emphasizes the generation of ideas and alternatives in an atmosphere of suspended judgment while contraction demands the use of judgment to identify the best idea/alternative. The presence of the group is considered to be a stimulating influence where people's ideas provoke each other, resulting in a chain of alternatives (Proctor 1999).

The modern popularization of brainstorming is attributed to Alex Osborn in the 1940s and 1950s (Proctor 1999). Osborn (1953) maintained that if brainstorming groups are to fulfill their mandate of finding the best solution to a problem, freewheeling of the imagination and deferment of judgment are critical prerequisites. Freewheeling of the imagination and deferment of judgment allow for an uninhibited generation of ideas including wild, exotic and unrealistic ones, without explanation, defensiveness, interruption and evaluation. In such a setting, brainstorming participants feel confident about sharing any thought that comes to their mind without fear of ridicule. Moreover, they also value all emerging ideas because they are fully aware that a solution can be triggered by any idea. Brainstorming goes beyond the mere generation of ideas by individual members. Participants attend to and build on each other's ideas in a variety of ways. Ideas shared during brainstorming not only inspire new thoughts and alternatives, but could also be fused together and/or improved upon. Evaluation and elaboration are the final stages of the brainstorming process.

Whether brainstorming actually increases creativity or simply increases the expression of ideas by lowering the standards for what is expressed is debatable. Nonetheless, since this approach is intended to lower the tendency to be critical during the idea elicitation stage, it assumes that, of the ideas that are expressed as a consequence of this relaxing of conventional restraints, some will prove to be solid when later subjected to critical evaluation. Moreover, the hope is that more good ideas will be generated by this process than by one in which people express only ideas that they have already evaluated critically (Nickerson 1999). Both Nickerson (1999) and Proctor (1999) cite evidence to show that brainstorming is effective in that groups using it have generated more and better ideas as compared to control groups not using it.

Ideally, a brainstorming session should comprise 10–12 people (including a leader/co-ordinator and a scribe) who are oriented to Osborn's principles of brainstorming outlined above. Prior to initiating the expansion/ideation stage, participants should agree upon the problem definition. Khandwalla (2004) emphasizes the significance of this as being the means by which the group gets direction for the rest of the session. In his view, brainstorming is not very fruitful unless the topic selected for brainstorming is specific. If the topic is vague, the brainstormers will carry different frames of reference and the ideas generated will have a diffused applicability. Khandwalla (2004) also suggests that once ideas have been generated, shortlisting of better ideas for more intensive investigation can be done by having each member of the group vote on the potential of each idea for solving the problem at hand. Sometimes the ideas can be grouped into classes and then each idea within a group may be voted upon. Sometimes it may be useful to formalize the criteria for assessing the potential of the ideas generated before the ideas are voted upon. Any reasonable system of voting will do, such as each voter indicating his/her three most preferred choices. If the ideas initially generated are very many, voting may have to be done more than once. That is to say, ideas voted the best in the initial round of voting may again be put to a vote to get a small number of high potential ideas. These ideas may then be taken up for much more intense scrutiny (Khandwalla 2004).

Proctor (1999) suggests a number of variants to Osborn's (1953) classical brainstorming process. "In stop-and-go brainstorming", for instance, the session is divided into segments. Rest periods are introduced every three to five minutes or so to allow participants to gather their thoughts and reflect over the ideas that have been recorded up to that point. Round-robin brainstorming entails that each person makes a contribution in turn. The "round" is repeated several times until it appears that ideas have dried up or until a fixed period of time has elapsed. In brainwriting, each person writes their ideas down on index cards, self-adhesive notes or slips of paper. Individuals can write their ideas down in a private, quiet place and share them later. Large groups find brainwriting useful because everyone gets to express his/her ideas completely and quickly.

Although brainstorming connotes a group activity, individuals can engage in a similar process by themselves (Khandwalla 2004, Nickerson 1999). Nickerson (1999) points out that, in a sense, one is brainstorming whenever one attempts to generate a set of possible courses of action or approaches to a problem, reserving criticism and evaluation of the list until it is relatively complete.

ACTIVITY SEQUENCE

(1) Nature Watch
(2) Recast
(3) Collective Contexts
(4) Brainstorming

NATURE WATCH

Instructor guidelines

Objectives

Using an ecological sensitivity activity that involves physical movement and group interaction serves as an energizing way of starting the workshop.

Time

Twenty minutes.

Procedure

(1) Divide the class into groups of six people each.

(2) Ask each group to walk around the institute campus/vicinity and ascertain in 10 minutes:

   (*a*) the number of different types of leaves in terms of colors and shapes.

   (*b*) the number of different types of flowers.

(3) At the end of 10 minutes, the group that comes back with the maximum number on both these counts is the winner and may be given a prize.

(4) Point out to the class that this was an exercise primarily to help them re-engage their ecological sensitivity while also setting the tone for the workshop.

The instructor may substitute "leaves" and "flowers" with any other observation linked to the surroundings.

RECAST

Instructor guidelines

Objectives

To experience others' (including non-human and inanimate forms) states of being, in the process becoming more aware of one's own self and challenging blocks and inhibitions.

Time

Seventy five minutes.

Material

Small strips of colored paper on which a recast option is printed (these should be as many as the number of participants and should be kept in a plastic/cardboard container).

A set of recast options is provided in the following pages though the instructor may generate his/her own options.

Procedure

(1) Each participant, in turn, has to come up and pick up a slip from the container. He/she has to play the part of the entity mentioned on the slip for two or three minutes, as per his/her own interpretation.

(2) At the end, a discussion may be held about the experience of becoming another entity and what this experience highlights in terms of learning about one's self, one's inhibitions, the world around, and the world from others' perspective. The link between this exercise and ideation and creativity may be brought out.

OPTIONS FOR RECAST

(1) Be a stone
(2) Be the Milky Way
(3) Be a snake
(4) Be a feather
(5) Be a rose
(6) Be grass
(7) Be a jungle
(8) Be a plane
(9) Be a plank of wood
(10) Be a blackboard
(11) Be shoe polish
(12) Be a spire

(13) Be a pencil
(14) Be a sparrow
(15) Be a flamingo
(16) Be a toddler
(17) Be a scorpion
(18) Be a cobweb
(19) Be a cycle
(20) Be Bill Gates
(21) Be a sea horse
(22) Be a flag
(23) Be the North Pole
(24) Be a coral
(25) Be a swing
(26) Be Steffi Graf
(27) Be Asia
(28) Be the Statue of Liberty
(29) Be Mount Everest
(30) Be John Lennon

COLLECTIVE CONTEXTS

Instructor guidelines

Objectives

To experience the influence of resources on creativity and to work on a creative task in a group (the experience gathered here is to be later contrasted with that gathered during brainstorming).

Time

Ninety minutes.

Material

(1) White chart paper—six sheets each for groups in the A category.
(2) Art materials including chart paper, glazed paper, crepe paper, paints, paint brushes, palettes, felt pens, crayons and color pencils—for groups in the B category.

(3) Stationery items including pencils, erasers, sharpeners, gum and scissors—for groups in the B category.

(4) Classrooms (one for each group) fitted with blackboard with chalk/whiteboard with markers and CD playing facility.

Procedure

(1) Divide the class into two groups of As and Bs. Further divide the As and Bs into smaller groups such that each group has about four or five people.

(2) Give each A group six sheets of white chart paper and each B group a set of the art and stationery materials listed above.

(3) Instruct them that, within 30 minutes, each group must independently create as many novel products as possible using only the materials provided to them.

(4) Groups may disperse to assigned classrooms so that they may work independently.

(5) Reassemble the groups after 30 minutes and allow them to share their products.

(6) Follow this up with a discussion on the impact of resources on their experience of being creative.

(7) Ask them to note down their experiences of group dynamics and to retain it.

BRAINSTORMING

Instructor guidelines

Objectives

To allow participants to experience brainstorming in its true form.

Time

Three hours.

Material

(1) Brainstorming worksheet (the number of copies must match the number of participants).

(2) Classrooms (one for each group) fitted with blackboard with chalk/whiteboard with markers and CD playing facility.

(3) Brainwriting package containing post-it notes, chart paper, cellotape and scissors (one package for each group).

(4) Art materials including chart paper, glazed paper, crepe paper, paints, paint brushes, palettes, felt pens, crayons and color pencils.

(5) Stationery items including pencils, erasers, sharpeners, gum and scissors.

(6) Magazines for pictures (magazines covering a variety of topics such as business, cookery, travel, fashion, and so on should be included to provide a range of pictures).

(7) Blackboard with chalk/whiteboard with markers.

(8) Picture and word force fitting trigger cards.

(9) Module 5 reflections sheet (the number of copies must match the number of participants).

(10) Module 5 reading handout (the number of copies must match the number of participants).

(11) Take-home assignment 5 (the number of copies must match the number of participants).

Procedure

(1) Explain the process of brainstorming to participants, highlighting classical brainstorming, round-robin style and brainwriting, and emphasizing the importance of suspension of judgment. Highlight how the incorporation of problem redefinition and ideation enhances the brainstorming process.

(2) Distribute the "Brainstorming" worksheet to participants, allowing them time to read it.

(3) Divide participants into groups and let them move in their groups to the assigned classroom, after picking up the brainwriting package.

(4) They may work on the assigned task for 120 minutes.

(5) Each group can then present their work and the instructor may give them feedback.

(6) The session may be completed by asking participants to reflect on and share their experience of the true process of brainstorming, contrasting it with the "Collective contexts" group activity and earlier experiences of brainstorming.

(7) Participants may then complete the Module 5 reflections sheet.

(8) Wrap up by outlining all that has been covered in the course, highlighting the relevance of creative thinking for organizational life (refer to the Prologue for this).

(9) Distribute take-home assignment 5 and Module 5 reading handout.

While a problem issue has been provided for the brainstorming activity, the instructor may select a problem/issue relevant to the participant group.

BRAINSTORMING

Worksheet

The note below describes the process of brainstorming. As you will see, brainstorming in its true form is quite distinct from its popular everyday usage. Following the proper procedures as outlined here is more effective to get a larger pool of creative ideas and to involve all group members. Hence when you use brainstorming today, make sure that you follow the correct steps.

Brainstorming: Guidelines and stages

Popularized by Alex Osborn (1953) as a tool to generate ideas, brainstorming involves three stages and some important ground rules.

(1) Examine the problem that has been given to you so that you understand it completely—you may use problem redefinition to aid this process. You may also challenge assumptions, do away with dominant ideas, change the entry point, and use reversal (as suggested by De Bono 1990).

(Please note that depending on the complexity of the problem, you may have to sub-divide it into parts and then deal with each part separately).

(2) In order to find solutions to the problem in a brainstorming session, you must first generate a pool of ideas from all group members without evaluating them. This involves three things:

(*a*) Ideas can be generated either by throwing up what comes to one's mind via imagination or through associations and random stimulation such that one can come up with wilder, more remote alternatives.

(*b*) All members of the group must contribute their ideas—the best way to do this is to adopt a round-robin style (Proctor 1999) where each person in turn is asked to make a contribution. The "round" is repeated several times until it appears that ideas have dried up or until a fixed period of time as elapsed. In case there are group members who are shy and inhibited, they may be asked to write their ideas (a process known as brainwriting [Proctor 1999]) and these are collected and added to the list generated by vocal members.

It is possible that during "a" and "b" above, the group runs out of ideas and may decide to take a break for a while and then return back to ideate together (the stop-and-go method [Proctor 1999]).

(*c*) During the ideating phase, the focus is on generating and pooling together ideas/alternatives, and hence to aid this process, judgment and evaluation are suspended as this may lead people to withhold their ideas if they feel that they may be ridiculed. Group members are expected to generate ideas without explaining them as this disrupts and inhibits the ideating process.

The aim of this phase is to generate as many novel ideas/alternatives as possible.

(3) After ideas are generated, then the process of finding solutions begins. The ideas/alternatives generated during brainstorming could be used as they are or they could be joined together or they could be further developed. They could inspire even more ideas/alternatives.

Often, the ideas are stimuli for solutions rather than solutions in themselves—hence they may have to undergo several refinements before they are amenable to application.

Please note that if you have sub-divided your problem into parts, you may apply these three stages to each part. You may then put the solutions for each sub-part together to get a composite solution/set of solutions.

Brainstorming groups (the ideal size should not be more than 10 members) generally appoint co-ordinators who ensure that the principles of brainstorming are appropriately followed as well as scribes who note down all the ideas being generated so that none are lost.

Clearly, the process described above differs from the popular practice of brainstorming where ideating and evaluating proceed concomitantly such that ideas are evaluated as they are generated with the result that initial plausible ideas are selected as solutions—there is no attempt to expand the pool of ideas as much as possible or to examine all the ways in/avenues by which the problem can be resolved. Under such circumstances, the search for the best possible solution is curtailed by the problem solving process itself.

Your task

Keeping in mind:

(a) the principles and stages of brainstorming.
(b) the ideational principles you have learnt so far, work in your groups on the following:

Internationalize your institute/organization to make it the most sought after business school/organization–employer in the world.

You have 120 minutes to complete this activity, and must come up with an original and elaborate solution.

MODULE 5 REFLECTIONS SHEET

Take a few minutes to recollect and note down your thoughts, feelings and actions on completion of today's workshop. While the questions below will give you some leads, they are not meant to be exhaustive.

About today's workshop

(1) Was this problem solving different to what I usually do? If yes, in what way?

(2) Was this different to the exercises I did last week? If yes, how and why? How do I feel about adopting such a problem solving style?

(3) How does this compare with my earlier experiences of brainstorming?

(4) How did I perform? Were there any factors like thoughts and feelings influencing me during the problem solving process—and how did they contribute to my task completion? What resources/supports (including intrapersonal ones) did I rely on during today's exercises? Was I conscious of what I was doing/ thinking/feeling during this time?

(5) How did I feel about working in a group as compared to working individually—what are my preferences and under what circumstances? What were the facilitating/constraining factors?

(6) What changes do I see in myself? Anything that I need to work on?

About myself

(1) How have my cognitive processes and sense of self changed over the last five weeks?

(2) Do I apply creative thinking techniques easily, without effort and consciousness, or do I have to remind myself to think creatively?

(3) Do I see value/benefit in the use of creative thinking?

(4) Which areas require further strengthening?

(5) In what way does Workshop 5 take this forward?

(6) Are there any areas that I need to work on/improve? If so, how do I plan to do so?

Wrap-up question

(1) Of all the techniques that I was exposed to during the five workshops, which one(s) was/were I most comfortable with, which one(s) did I enjoy using (may not be the same as the ones I was comfortable with)? In respect of which techniques do I see potential of being used further/getting more familiar with?

(2) Am I more aware of my cognitive processes as well as aspects of myself and how these affect my ability to think creatively?

(3) What changes have I observed in myself/my way of thinking since Workshop 1? In what aspects of my life have these changes taken place? What facilitates and what inhibits these changes?

(4) Are these changes influencing my everyday life/activities/thinking?

(5) How can I ensure that these changes remain with me over time?

(6) Which areas require further strengthening?

(7) How do I ensure that these skills remain internalized as a part of my self?

TAKE-HOME ASSIGNMENT 5

This assignment must be completed and submitted within two weeks. You may use extra sheets as required.

Drawing on your learnings in the course so far, develop an innovative and elaborate business plan in any area of your choice.

Reflect on your experience of completing the above assignment. Prepare a write-up describing your creative process including being creative, why/how you selected this project, what mental processes helped or hindered your creative thinking ability, what techniques you engaged to aid you, the blocks and facilitators which you experienced, any conclusions which you can derive about your own creative strengths and weaknesses, and so on. Integrate as many concepts as you can in the write-up.

References

Ainsworth-Land, V. 1982. 'Imaging and Creativity', *Journal of Creative Behavior*, 16(1): 5–28.

Amabile, T.M. 1983. *The Social Psychology of Creativity*. New York: Springer-Verlag.

———. 1996a. *Creativity and Innovation in Organisations*. Harvard Business School Note 9-396-239. Boston, MA: Harvard Business School Press.

———. 1996b. *Managing for Creativity*. Harvard Business School Note 9-396-271. Boston, MA: Harvard Business School Press.

Amabile, T.M. and E. Tighe. 1993. 'Questions of Creativity', in J. Brockman (ed.), *Creativity*, pp. 7–27. New York: Simon & Schuster.

Arieti, S. 1976. *Creativity: The Magic Synthesis*. New York: Basic Books.

Baron, R.A. and D. Byrne. 2004. *Social Psychology*. New Delhi: Pearson.

Crawford, R.P. 1954. *The Techniques of Creative Thinking: How to Use Your Ideas to Achieve Success*. New York: Hawthorne.

Cropley, A.J. 1992. *More Ways than One: Fostering Creativity*. Norwood, NJ: Ablex Publishing.

———. 1999. 'Definitions of Creativity', in M. Runco and S. Pritzer (eds), *Encyclopedia of Creativity*, Volume 1, pp. 511–24. London: Academic Press.

Csikszentmihalyi, M. 1988. 'Society, Culture, and Person: A Systems View of Creativity', in R.J. Sternberg (ed.), *The Nature of Creativity*, pp. 325–339. New York: Cambridge University Press.

———. 1996. *Creativity*. New York: HarperCollins.

Csikszentmihalyi, M. and K. Rathunde. 1998. 'The Development of the Person: An Experiential Perspective on the Ontogenesis of Psychological Complexity', in R.M. Lerner (ed.), *Handbook of Child Psychology*, Volume 1, pp. 635–84. New York: John Wiley.

Csikszentmihalyi, M. and K. Sawyer. 1995. 'Creative Insight: The Social Dimension of a Solitary Moment', in R.J. Sternberg and J.E. Davidson (eds), *The Nature of Insight*, pp. 329–61. Cambridge, MA: MIT Press.

Dacey, J. 1999. 'Concept of Creativity: A History', in M. Runco and S. Pritzer (eds), *Encyclopedia of Creativity*, Volume 1, pp. 309–22. London: Academic Press.

Damanpour, F. and W.M. Evan. 1984. 'Organisational Innovation and Performance: The Problem of Organizational Lag', *Administrative Science Quarterly*, 29: 392–409.

Davis, G.A. 1999. 'Barriers to Creativity and Creative Attitudes', in M. Runco and S. Pritzer (eds), *Encyclopedia of Creativity*, Volume 1. London: Academic Press.

De Bono, E. 1990. *Lateral Thinking*. London: Penguin.

———. 2000. *Six Thinking Hats*. London: Penguin.

DeGraff, J. and K.A. Lawrence. 2002. *Creativity at Work: Developing the Right Practices to Make Innovation Happen*. New Delhi: Wiley India.

Epstein, R. 1999. 'Generativity Theory', in M. Runco and S. Pritzer (eds), *Encyclopedia of Creativity*, Volume 1, pp. 759–66. London: Academic Press.

Fasko Jr., D. 1999. 'Associative Theory', in M. Runco and S. Pritzer (eds), *Encyclopedia of Creativity*, Volume 1, pp. 135–39. London: Academic Press.

Feldman, D.H. 1999. 'The Development of Creativity', in R.J. Sternberg (ed.), *Handbook of Creativity*, pp. 169–86. New York: Cambridge University Press.

Finke, R.A., T.B. Ward and S.M. Smith. 1992. *Creative Cognition: Theory, Research, and Applications*. Cambridge, MA: MIT Press.

Freeman, J. 1983. 'Emotional Problems of the Gifted Child', *Journal of Child Psychology and Psychiatry*, 24(5): 481–85.

Frensch, P.A. and R.J. Sternberg. 1989. 'Expertise and Intelligent Thinking: When is it Worse to Know Better?', in R.J. Sternberg (ed.), *Advances in the Psychology of Human Intelligence*, Volume 5, pp. 157–58. Hillsdale, NJ: Erlbaum.

Gardner, H. 1993. 'Seven Creators of the Modern Era', in J. Brockman (ed.), *Creativity*, pp. 28–47. New York: Simon & Schuster.

Gordon, W.J. 1961. *Synectics*. New York: Harper and Row.

Goswami, A. 1999. 'Quantum Theory of Creativity', in M. Runco and S. Pritzer (eds), *Encyclopedia of Creativity*, Volume 2, pp. 491–500. London: Academic Press.

Guilford, J.P. 1950. 'Creativity', *American Psychologist*, 5(9): 444–54.

Hailey, V.H. 2001. 'Breaking the Mould? Innovation as a Strategy for Corporate Renewal', *International Journal of Human Resource Management*, 12(7): 1126–40.

Harvard Business School. 2003. *Managing Creativity and Innovation*. Cambridge, MA: HBSP.

Hennessey, B.A. and T.M. Amabile. 1988. 'The Conditions of Creativity', in R.J. Sternberg (ed.), *The Nature of Creativity*, pp. 11–38. New York: Cambridge University Press.

Hicks, M.J. 1991. *Problem Solving in Business and Management*. London: Chapman & Hall.

Khandwalla, P.N. 2003. *Corporate Creativity: The Winning Edge*. New Delhi: Tata McGraw-Hill.

———. 2004. *Lifelong Creativity*. New Delhi: Tata McGraw-Hill.

Koestler, A. 1964. *The Act of Creation*. London: Hutchinson.

Kuhn, T. 1962. *The Structure of Scientific Revolutions*. Chicago: University of Chicago Press.

Kurtzberg, T.R. and T.M. Amabile. 2000–2001. 'From Guilford to Creative Synergy: Opening the Black Box of Team-level Creativity', *Creativity Research Journal*, 13(3 and 4): 285–94.

Lubart, T.I. 1999. 'Componential Models', in M. Runco and S. Pritzer (eds), *Encyclopedia of Creativity*, Volume 1, pp. 295–300. London: Academic Press.

Mackinnon, D.W. 1970. 'Creativity: A Multi-faceted Phenomenon', in J.D. Roslansky (ed.), *Creativity*, pp. 17–32. London: North Holland.

Martinsen, O. and G. Kaufmann. 1999. 'Cognitive Style and Creativity', in M. Runco and S. Pritzer (eds), *Encyclopedia of Creativity*, Volume 1, pp. 273–82. London: Academic Press.

Mayer, R.E. 1999. 'Problem solving', in M. Runco and S. Pritzer (eds), *Encyclopedia of Creativity*, Volume 2, pp. 437–47. London: Academic Press.

McCrae, R.R. 1999. 'Consistency of Creativity Across the Life-span', in M. Runco and S. Pritzer (eds), *Encyclopedia of Creativity*, Volume 1, pp. 361–66. London: Academic Press.

Mednick, S.A. 1962. 'The Associative Basis of Creative Process', *Psychological Review*, 69: 220–32.

Nickerson, R.S. 1999. 'Enhancing Creativity', in R.J. Sternberg (ed.), *Handbook of Creativity*, pp. 392–430. New York: Cambridge University Press.

Noronha, E. 2005. *Ethnicity in Industrial Organisations*. New Delhi: Rawat.

Ohlsson, S. 1992. 'Information Processing Explanation of Insight and Related Phenomena', in M.T. Keane and K.J. Gilhooly (eds), *Advances in Psychology of Thinking*, Volume 1, pp. 1–44. New York: Harvester Wheatsheat.

Osborn, A. 1953. *Applied Imagination*. New York: Scribner's.

Plucker, J.A. and M.A. Runco. 1999. 'Enhancement of Creativity', in M. Runco and S. Pritzer (eds), *Encyclopedia of Creativity*, Volume 1, pp. 669–75. London: Academic Press.

Prince, G.M. 1968. 'Operational Mechanisms of Synectics', *Journal of Creative Behaviour*, 2(1): 1–13.

Proctor, T. 1999. *Creative Problem Solving for Managers*. London: Routledge.

Ripple, R.E. 1999. 'Teaching Creativity', in M. Runco and S. Pritzer (eds), *Encyclopedia of Creativity*, Volume 2, pp. 629–38. London: Academic Press.

Rothenberg, A. 1999a. 'Homospatial Process', in M. Runco and S. Pritzer (eds), *Encyclopedia of Creativity*, Volume 1, pp. 831–35. London: Academic Press.

———. 1999b. 'Janusian Process', in M. Runco and S. Pritzer (eds), *Encyclopedia of Creativity*, Volume 2, pp. 103–08. London: Academic Press.

Runco, M.A. 1999a. 'Contrarianism', in M. Runco and S. Pritzer. (eds), *Encyclopedia of Creativity*, Volume 1, pp. 367–71. London: Academic Press.

———. 1999b. 'Divergent Thinking', in M. Runco and S. Pritzer (eds), *Encyclopedia of Creativity*, Volume 1, pp. 577–82. London: Academic Press.

Seifert, C.M., D.E. Meyer, N. Davidson, A.L. Patalano and I. Yuniv. 1995. 'Demystification of Cognitive Insight: Opportunistic Assimilation and the Prepared Mind Perspective', in R.J. Sternberg and J.E. Davidson (eds), *The Nature of Insight*, pp. 65–124. Cambridge, MA: MIT Press.

Simonton, D.K. 1984. *Genius, Creativity and Leadership: Historiometric Inquiries*. Cambridge, MA: Harvard University Press.

Singer, J.L. 1999. 'Imagination', in M. Runco and S. Pritzer (eds), *Encyclopedia of Creativity*, Volume 2, pp. 13–25. London: Academic Press.

Smith, S.M. 1995. 'Getting Into and Out of Mental Ruts', in R.J. Sternberg and J.E. Davidson (eds), *The Nature of Insight*, pp. 121–49. Cambridge, MA: MIT Press.

Smith, S.M. and R.A. Dodds. 1999. 'Incubation', in M. Runco and S. Pritzer (eds), *Encyclopedia of Creativity*, Volume 2, pp. 39–43. London: Academic Press.

Sternberg, R.J. and T.I. Lubart. 1991. 'An Investment Theory of Creativity and its Development', *Human Development*, 34(1): 1–32.

———. 1996. 'Investing in Creativity', *American Psychologist*, 51(7): 677–88.

———. 1999. 'The Concept of Creativity: Prospects and Paradigm', in R.J. Sternberg (ed.), *Handbook of Creativity*, pp. 3–15. New York: Cambridge University Press.

Sternberg, R.J., J.E. Pretz and J.C. Kaufman. 2003. 'Types of Innovations', in L.V. Shavinina (ed.), *International Handbook on Innovation*, pp. 158–69. Oxford, UK: Elsevier.

Tauber, E.M. 1972. 'HIT: Heuristic Ideation Technique—A Systematic Procedure for New Product Search', *Journal of Marketing*, 36(1): 58–61.

Torrance, E.P. 1974. *Torrance Tests of Creative Thinking*. Lexington, M.A.: Personnel Press.

Van de Ven, A.H. 1986. 'Central Problems in the Management of Innovation', *Management Science*, 32(5): 590–607.

Wallas, G. 1926. *The Art of Thought*. London: Jonathan Cape.

Ward, T.B., S.M. Smith and R.A. Finke. 1999. 'Creativity, the Self and the Environment', in R.J. Sternberg (ed.), *Handbook of Creativity*, pp. 189–212. New York: Cambridge University Press.

Weisberg, R.W. 2006. *Creativity: Understanding Innovation in Problem Solving, Science, Invention and the Arts*. USA: Wiley & Sons, Inc.

West, M.A. and T. Rickards. 1999. 'Innovation', in M. Runco and S. Pritzer (eds), *Encyclopedia of Creativity*, Volume 2, pp. 45–55. London: Academic Press.

Williams, W.M. and T.L. Yang. 1999. 'Organizational Creativity', in R.J. Sternberg (ed.), *Handbook of Creativity*, pp. 373–91. New York: Cambridge University Press.

Zwicky, F. 1948. *Discovery, Invention, Research through the Morphological Approach*. New York: Macmillan.

Premilla D'Cruz is Assistant Professor of Organizational Behavior at Indian Institute of Management (IIM), Ahmedabad, where she teaches Micro Organizational Behavior, Macro Organizational Behavior and Creativity. A Ph.D. in Social Sciences from the Tata Institute of Social Sciences, Mumbai, Dr D'Cruz's research interests include emotions in organizations, self and identity, organizational control and ICTs and organizations. She has published *Family Care in HIV/AIDS: Exploring Lived Experience* (SAGE) and *In Sickness and in Health: The Family Experience of HIV/AIDS in India* (Stree), apart from numerous international papers and presentations. She has previously held faculty positions at Indian Institute of Technology (IIT) Kanpur and IIM Kozhikode.

50
2